D1374618

*THE
UNSINKABLE
KILCULLEN*

THE UNSINKABLE KILCULLEN

Across the Atlantic by Inflatable
—and Other Ways to Get Wet

ENDA O'COINEEN

THE BODLEY HEAD

LONDON

British Library Cataloguing
in Publication Data

O'Coineen, Enda Pádraig
The unsinkable Kilcullen: across the
Atlantic by inflatable—and other ways
to get wet.
1. Voyages and travels—1951–
2. Inflatable boats 3. North Atlantic
Ocean
I. Title
910'.091631   G465

ISBN 0-370-31119-1

Printed in Ireland for
The Bodley Head Ltd
32 Bedford Square, London WC1B 3EL
by Ireland Afloat Magazine
Set in Bembo
by Ireland Afloat Magazine

First published 1987

Contents

To the women in my life:
the Lady Suzanna,
girlchilds Roisin and
Aisling,
and Mum

List of Illustrations

29. Sea trials and sail balance
30. The cockpit, *Kilcullen (III)*
31. At the Guinness Stand, Earl's Court, with Richard Branson
32. Receiving the Black Bush Whiskey Award, Piccadilly, London

(Drawn by Geoff Page)

Author's Foreword

LUCK is one of the most peculiar and most abused four-lettered words that I know of. Several times it has been said that I've been steeped and rich in the stuff that luck is made from. Perhaps. Certainly in terms of what I have been fortunate in achieving to date I have surely been blessed with more than my fair share of God's allocated luck quota. They say it is an Irish trait. I'd like to think so, but it is not as simple as that.

You make luck. Like opportunity, you go out and grab it.

Kathleen Hehir, living between the rocks in Connemara on the western seaboard of Europe, is convinced that the reason I'll never drown is because I am a Seanás, and a totally separate source, my Auntie Della in Galway town, backs this up. According to some obscure West of Ireland tradition, a Seanás is a person who has a gap between the two front teeth. Maybe I've been lucky to be born a Seanás?

As I crawled around on top of the bottom of my 16ft inflatable boat, some 700 miles east of St John's, Newfoundland, in violent breaking seas—seas in which rocks would float—there is little doubt that exposure and hypothermia would have struck far swifter than my Seanás could have stopped me from drowning. On my second attempt to beat this stretch of the North Atlantic, yet again I was in serious difficulties upside down on a ruthless ocean fighting for my very existence.

This was it. Surely my luck had run dry. I had vowed once before never to put myself in that situation again; but here I was battling the elements all over again. 'Never', I have learned the hard way, is a word which you should never use.

But this was my own doing and responsibility. As a child from virtually day one, I have always been adventurous and, at times, considered wild. People would always seem to me to be continually finding more reasons for not doing something than getting on with it. The Enda O'Coineen approach, which has developed into a simple philosophy, is that if you've got something to do, go out and do it, regardless of what people think—provided that you do not cause any unnecessary hardship or inconvenience in the process.

In this book I welcome the opportunity to share my adventures, relating them in print. I trust that you enjoy it as much as I have in completing it. Television cameras may come, newsprint may roll but a book is forever. The former being like a one-night stand with a nice woman—you make the best of it—the latter being more permanent, like getting married: you make it good to stand the test of time.

Many have helped, not least being Suzanna for being patient and encouraging while I made love to the typewriter, and Guido Waldman of my publishers for his guidance and interest.

During my travels and adventures I have been fortunate to meet many wonderful friends, individuals and companies who have supported me in my endeavours and have helped along the way (some even unwittingly); to them I say thanks. Hopefully, I have managed to include all in the Acknowledgements.

Finally, having heard myself described as an uncontrolled flying missile going through life, I have spent this while trying to figure out whether this was an insult or a compliment. Always one to be positive, I have opted for the latter. Now I am not so sure. However on entering a new era and having helped create a wonderful family from being a twinkle in somebody's eye, that uncontrolled flying missile has landed.

Let us not be saddened though, it will be launched again, but this time in a controlled manner and never in a rubber dinghy.

Enda O'Coineen
—Ireland, February 1987

Acknowledgements

It gives me great pleasure to list and say thanks to the following who have helped or supported me in some way:

ORGANIZATIONS

Allied Irish Banks
Allweather Marine—Alan Kemp
Arklow Shipping—*Arklow View*
BIM—Dr Tony Meaney
B. J. Marine—Bernard Gallagher
The British Government
The *Daily Express*
Downer Sails
Galway Advertiser—Ronnie O'Gorman
Galway Bay Sailing Club
Guinness Harp Corporation, New York
Heron Group—Steve Kenward and Mike Nickol
Humber Inflatables
Ireland Afloat Magazine
Irish Distillers
The Irish Press Group

Kelvin Hughes— Michael White
McGarvey's Bar—Mike Ashford
Maritime Institute of Ireland
Marmaduke's Bar
Motorboat & Yachting
National Yacht Club
Nautech—Autohelm
Ocean Hotel—Brendan Gallagher
Plastimo—Brian Braine
Priory Imports—Tony Duffey
RTE
Seafarer—Colin Minor
Soundings—Jack Turner
Union Chandlery—John Wallace
Watson & Jameson Sails
Western Marine—Ted Magee
Zodiac of North America
The Irish Times.

INDIVIDUALS

Norman Barry
Annmarie & Peter Bowring
Bill Buckley

Richard Burrows
The people of Cat Island (Bahamas)

Mike Connolly
Tim Pat Coogan
Michael Cullen
Tim Curtis
Tom Di Laura
Peter Dix
Elinor Emerson
Keith Emerson
Derek Garvey
Captain Eric Healy
Peter Hudson
Pete Jackson
Robin Knox Johnston
Tristan Jones
King Juan II
Aideen Kennedy
Des Burke Kennedy
Commander Bill King
Tom Lawlor
Judy Lawson
Leslie Lee
Brian & Onora Lynch
Don Macauley
Peter Mason

Grainne Ui Mhaitiu
Dirk Nauta
William and Georgina Nixon
Dr Donie O'Beirne
Professor Sean O'Beirn
David O'Brien
Micheail O'Cinneide
Kevin O'Farrell
Pol O'Foighil
Peter Phillips
Dag Pike
Jim Poole
Pierce Purcell
Arthur & Allister Rumball
Andrew Sanford
Don & Lori Shurtleff
Eileen Sugrue
Dick Warner
Crew and passengers on the
    West Indian mailboat, 17
    March 1980
Frank Woods
Jon & Jennifer Wynne Tyson

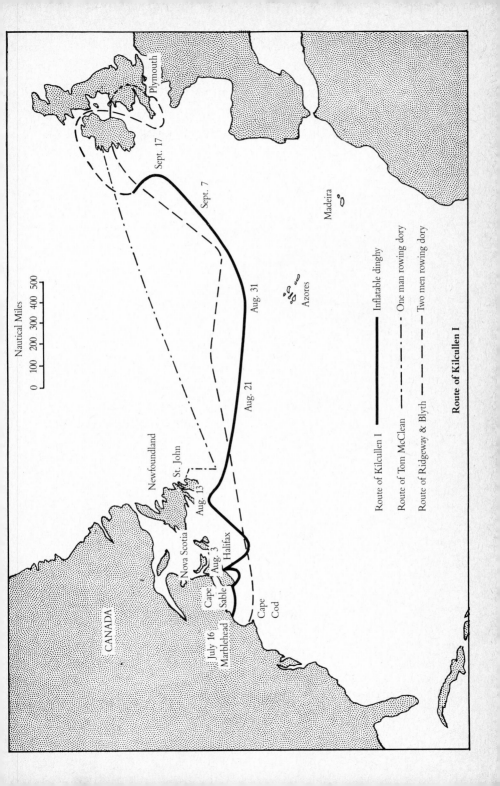

Nautical Miles

0   100 200 300 400 500

Plymouth

Sept. 17

Sept. 7

Madeira

Aug. 31

Azores

Aug. 21

Newfoundland

St. John

Aug. 13

Nova Scotia

Cape   Aug. 3

Sable   Halifax

Cape
Cod

CANADA

July 16
Marblehead

Route of Kilcullen I ————————— Inflatable dinghy

Route of Tom McClean —·—·—·—·— One man rowing dory

Route of Ridgeway & Blyth ————— Two men rowing dory

Route of Kilcullen I

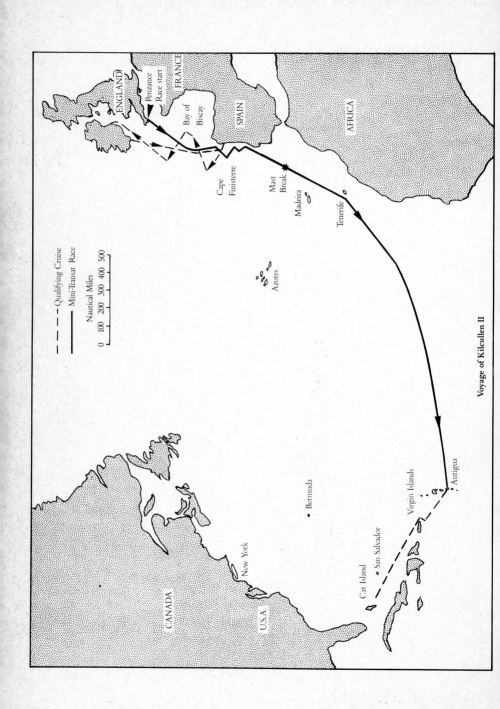

Voyage of Kilcullen II

CANADA

U.S.A.

New York

Bermuda

Cat Island

San Salvador

Virgin Islands

Antigua

ENGLAND

FRANCE

Penzance
Race start

Bay of
Biscay

SPAIN

AFRICA

Cape
Finisterre

Mast
Break

Madeira

Tenerife

Azores

- - - Qualifying Cruise

——— Mini-Transat Race

Nautical Miles

0 100 200 300 400 500

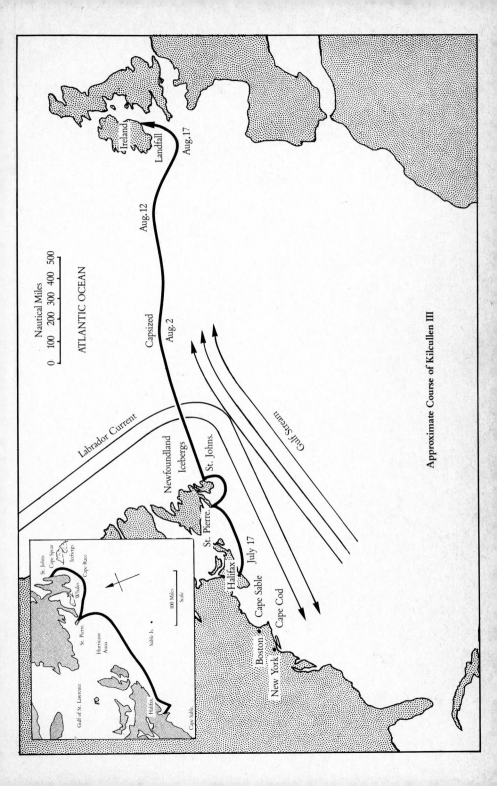

Approximate Course of Kilcullen III

PROLOGUE

Boston 1977

WHILE GOD-FEARING, I was not particularly religious at that time, but it seemed natural to go to church. Every insurance, spiritual or otherwise, made sense. Conflicting thoughts about the whole business were constantly turning over in my mind as I sat alone; was I helping to advance the frontiers of science and marine safety or was I a rip-roaring lunatic? Yet nothing—not even a convoy of steam rollers, a lifelong supply of beer, or the Pope himself, could stop the departure at this stage; even if I was only 21 years of age.

The atmosphere was quiet and meditative. The silent shuffle of feet and the flotilla of little old ladiew with purple hair and high-rimmed glasses mixed with local society dressed in their sunday best. It was an old church with a high roof and hard benches: foam kneelers had not yet arrived in Marblehead, Massachusetts. The ornate marble altar and statues in abundance for worship were unnatural. The prayers were boring, and I was anxious to be on my way from this beautiful little seaport outside Boston.

After Mass I innocently asked the young curate, Father Powell, to come and bless the *Kilcullen* before departure. He kindly obliged, but his Roman collar nearly dropped around his ankles when he cast eyes over the tiny rubber boat and learned of the proposed voyage across the North Atlantic. Until then I had been keeping a low profile in case the local Coast Guard should take it in their heads to stop me going. Besides, my mother was expecting me to ring from the Aran Islands, over on her side of the ocean, but she did not have an idea as to how her nomadic son intended getting there.

A small crowd had gathered on the quayside. Though caught unprepared, the resourceful priest produced a beautiful nautical prayer from his book for the simple blessing ceremony.

1

'God bless this ship and all who sail in her,' he concluded.

A young boy by the name of Macaulay lent me a large roll of heavy-duty duct tape which was to prove very useful for repairs. His father never let him forget the loan and it was to take me eight years before I could return it.

Photographs of that jolly departure show me looking like a cross between a Trappist monk and your average local friendly village madman. I had not looked in a mirror since my hair was cut in the middle of the previous night. I was therefore unaware that I looked as if somebody had put a bowl over my long hair and had cut around the sides—as indeed somebody had done in Mike Connolly's darkly lit shebeen under his home at Watertown in Boston suburbia.

Mike Connolly was also on the quayside to see the *Kilcullen* off. The man's missing hands, which had been substituted by steel claws, in no way detracted from the "presence" which he exuded. In mighty form, he too had recovered from the send-off party the night before, which had resulted in the bowl cut hairstyle. In truth I could not have cared less since there were few people to notice it where I was going. Mind you, that crazy cut might just explain why the fishermen I later encountered en route seemed a little reluctant to approach me.

I had first met Mike on arrival in the U.S. for the 1976 bi-centennial celebrations when we emptied all of our tea leaves into the harbour to mark the Boston Tea Party. He is one of Ireland's priceless exports to America. He has left Ireland, but Ireland has not left him; or to put it another way, you can take the man from the bog but you can't take the bog from the man. A colourful and sincere Connemara man, he recalled the losing of his hands in a shoe assembly plant not long after arriving as an emigrant to the New World. The work was hard, fast and on a piece rate.

'It was like a nightmare,' says he. 'Without warning the massive guillotine shot down and my arms were the other side.' The last he saw of them, he added, was on their voyage away on a conveyor belt, among the half-made shoes. 'My mind kept moving my hands but they were gone. I remember the horrible sight of my Claddagh wedding ring disappearing on one of my dead fingers. Gone for ever. It was awful.'

That accident was particularly tragic because Mike had been

musically gifted with his hands. Happily the story of his rehabilitation and support from his wife, Trudy, is a remarkable one.
Mike is now employed in the computer business and even
manages to play the harmonica with style in his own Irish traditional Ceili band. Now, by way of total contradiction to Mike's
loss, the misfortunes I was then getting immersed in were entirely
my choice.

Tom DiLaura then showed up. Despite his big heart, bless
him, it was difficult for him to forgive me for the sticky beer
which I had poured over him the night before. He had remained
in his tent, hung-over and furious, but now I was forgiven.

Then it was 'farewell' and away went the *Kilcullen* and her
intrepid captain. The idle joke, which had developed into an idea
and then into a bet with myself, was now becoming a reality:
the Atlantic by inflatable boat.

1

In with a bang—Galway 1959

MY EARLIEST childhood memory is of coming around after being out cold. I had been knocked over by a car while playing with a toy truck on the quiet, twisty road that ran past my house into Galway town. I remember coming around and staring into dozens of eyes obstructing my view of the sky. 'He's not dead at all,' my sister shouted as I wondered what all the fuss was about. Nevertheless my four-year-old head hurt, though I was delighted by all of the attention. As one of a family of three boys and five girls and a neighbourhood bursting with children, you had to be very different to attract attention. I went around for the rest of the day delighted not to be dead, with a sort of pride at having survived, but I had often wondered as a child what it would feel like to be dead.

'Keep that sort of carry-on up and the Devil will get his hands on you forever and you'll roast in hell,' my older sister barked out with real conviction, sending a shiver down through my little spine. Maybe being dead would not be so interesting after all. But I had become a survivor.

Going to school for the first time also left its mark on me. While most children are excited by the prospect, my reaction was totally the opposite. I was stubborn and refused flatly to go. This was probably brought on by horror stories I had heard about school from older children. Not even sweets could buy co-operation; indeed one day I recall doing a heavy number in my trousers— the smell and disruption being sufficient to get me sent home.

Contrariness was my hallmark. Tell Enda to do something and he would invariably do the opposite. Tell me that black was not white and to be sure I'd set out to prove that black was as white as can be. Other mothers in the neighbourhood were somewhat afraid of me, one in particular, ever since I had split

5

her son's head open with a snowball. My snowballs at this time were no ordinary affairs; they generally had a nice stone in the middle. Every time that particular lady saw me coming out to 'play', her timid son—or so he seemed to me at that time—was promptly taken indoors. The wee lad liked to copy me, even if he could not quite do it properly. One time he attempted to follow me along the top of a nine-foot wall. He fell, I made it, and my mother received yet another angry complaint.

Then came the 'bomb' era.

In my early 'teens there was a period when I simply got a big kick out of making loud bangs. The bomb season would normally start in the neighbourhood about two months before Hallowe'en and keep erupting until well into the New Year. At first we were not so good at it; however, with age our standards and bang quality improved until finally we resorted to exploding the big ones underwater—the bangs were so loud. An odd time, a dead salmon or trout might float to the surface after the under-water explosions.

The basis for the bombs we made in our secret gang was weed-killer. In more scientific terms it is known as sodium chlorate. Older friends were persuaded to buy or steal this for us from McDonagh's hardware store in Galway town. This stuff, mixed with sugar and stuffed into copper pipes, acquired from local building sites, made a deadly combination. Firstly, one end of the copper tube (the dimensions of which determined the size of the bang) would be hammered tight and doubled over to act as a seal. A hole would be hammered in the centre, usually with a nail, to provide a place for the fuse; then our gun-powder-like mixture was packed in tight and the other end was hammered flat. In the early bombs we would have a trail of explosive leading from the pipe. You lit this and you ran like hell. Later we acquired a special fuse that would work underwater. By mixing sulphur and other chemicals, concoctions learned from a big fat book entitled *Fortunes in Formulas,* our bomb material later approached gunpowder with its quick igniting properties, and made even louder bangs.

How none of these bombs ever exploded prematurely while I and my pals hammered away defies explanation. We were lucky. Perhaps we were sobered a little when we listened to a lad who lost a hand when a copper pipe bomb exploded as he was sealing it with a hammer.

Again I was a survivor. I grew up and moved on while one of my former young partners graduated to gelignite bangs and the Irish Republican Army.

Drink was also another source of great fascination, probably because it was something that was strictly prohibited. Our first attempts at getting drunk were disastrous and very sickening. Word had it that some aspirins mixed in with Coke would do the trick. I remember going down a back laneway with loads of Coke and aspirins, then gobbling half a bottle down and drinking the Coke like a thirsty Arab. It simply didn't work and I was sick for a week.

Cider, of course, did the trick. It generated a sort of mad drunken behaviour, and to make it last, the trick we learned from the local tinkers (or itinerants as they are now called), was to line our stomachs with dry bread to soak up the cider to keep the alcohol in our systems for longer. One time we attempted to make our own cider, again using the *Fortunes in Formulas* book. This involved deviating some bags of apples from the local Franciscan monastery and squeezing them to make and ferment the cider. Again this proved sickening; the end product was alcoholic but poison.

In retrospect, it is not as if I was badly brought up or that I was a low sort of youth. My dear mother would probably be horrified to read the foregoing. It is just that if there was anything that needed trying out I was the one to do it. Had drugs been available then, as is the sad case today, I would have undoubtedly tried them too.

The sea too was a drug. Talk of ships and the ocean always fascinated me. The River Corrib, which flows from the great Lough Corrib and the Connemara Mountains, meandered its way past our family home down into the sea. Two miles over the hill are Galway Bay, the Aran Islands and then the wild Atlantic Ocean with nothing more until America. Little did I then suspect that I'd be swept into a personal affair with this turbulent sea on inflatable boats.

Over a hundred years ago going to sea for pleasure from Galway would have been very odd indeed. Even when I was a child—and that's not so long ago—the concept of going to sea for pleasure was an alien one, though nowadays it is no longer so odd. Galway is a port which has seen massive emigration since the tragic Famine in Ireland, when starvation followed by disease and massive emigration reduced the country's population from eight to four million. The lucky ones were those who got away to America in old ships, making Galway just a one-way port. The emigrant boats were called 'Coffin Ships' as those that didn't founder usually docked in the New World with considerably fewer passengers than they had started out with.

My great-great-grandfather, Cormac—a name styled after a great High King of Ireland—was one of the countless numbers who lined the quays of Galway to sail in the dreaded ships for the New World, where the streets were believed to be paved with gold. His seafaring was simply a means to an end and, it is said, he bore no love for the ocean, which on reflection is not surprising.

Leaving Ireland then was just like dying from the perspective of those left at home, as emigrants rarely returned; for this reason emigrants were given a 'wake', a massive celebration where the whiskey flowed before the unfortunate body was deposited in the ground—or in the case of my forebear, on the ship. In this respect old man O'Coineen was like Finnegan, the man immortalized in the song for having returned to life at his own wake: 'You're spillin' whiskey around like blazes, by the thundering Jasus do you think I'm dead?'

By all accounts, Cormac found his way to Alaska and, while many perished, he survived the Great Winter there before going on down to the wild West of California. Here he struck it rich. Not a fortune, mind you, but enough gold to pay his fare home. To boot, his pockets were sufficiently lined to be able to afford a wife and several children (in his late forties, he was no spring chicken). It also proved enough to start a family business which included everything from a pub to a grocery store and bakery. The pub still stands.

'How dare you say that your family were illiterate? Some things are best forgotten,' a relative reprimanded me one time when we were discussing great-great-grandfather.

I bear no shame, and why should I? Indeed I'm rather proud of this fact. Despite all his travels Cormac could neither read nor write, which was the case with ninety per cent of the population at that time. Because of English rule at the time in Ireland, names that were too Irish sounding, for convenience as much as anything else, were translated into the closest English equivalent, which was often very inaccurate. The name of a business had to be in English on a shop front. In Galway city on one street the names Salmon, Badger, Hare and Rabbitt are all examples of very fine Irish surnames badly translated into English. Very often they were later translated back again into bad Irish, far removed from the original.

Our family pub became known officially as Rabbitts, though the Irish name, O'Coinin or O'Coineen, continued to be used by some members of the family. This old pub in Foster Street, now run by Murtagh Rabbitt and his son John, pulls the best pint of stout in all of Ireland. Nevertheless, the Irish version of the surname which is spelt in various ways, remains correct.

Being the eldest in his family my father was left the pub. However, having grown up in the pub, he was anxious to be out of it and the hazy world of alcohol. His father before him had died of lung cancer from the atmosphere, though he never smoked himself. Also there was always the danger of becoming your own best customer. So, while his younger brother Murtagh got on with making a great success of the pub, my father followed his own career in construction, dedicated himself to his family and worked himself into an early grave.

Father was mad about fishing and had a great interest in boats; he teamed up with a small local builder to form Hickey Boats, noted as a very progressive company in its day with several interesting new designs, displays at the London Boat Show and so forth.

I was mad about boats, too. Sailing beat school any day, I thought, and I planned to run away to sea. My interest in everything that floated was more than just the physical aspect of being on the water. It represented freedom, adventure and travel to faraway places. The sea, said I, was an education. The Jesuit fathers are a better one, said my parents.

At school with the Jesuit fathers I joined the rowing club and was coxswain for many schoolboy crews. Around that time in Galway, word got out that a group was coming together to form a sailing club where none had existed previously. The meeting took place in Corinthians Rugby Football Club. I went along and was somewhat nervous among the strangers and older men, but somebody bought me a pint and I knew that I had really grown up. It was decided to buy two Mirror sailing dinghies, and that was the meeting at which Galway Bay Sailing Club was founded. Our first boat was in fact a Mirror dinghy, which was called *Crubeen*—pig's foot—and it was launched and sailed with great fanfare. I was to spend summers working as a sailing instructor and gained my first offshore sailing experience on board the *Asgard,* a sail training ketch then under the command of Eric Healy, and famous in modern Irish history for gun running. The boat is now on display in Kilmainham jail, which has been turned into a museum.

Back at school, my days were filled with trouble and mischief. Life looked strange to me then as an adolescent, and I still think of it as a never-ending tightrope walk. 'A trouble maker, a biteen daft,' was how one of the priests described me. 'A fly in the ointment,' he added.

If nothing else, I was stubborn. In retrospect I was really rebelling against authority of any description. On several occasions I was 'expelled', though each time ways were found to get me taken back. But one time it was three months before my parents found out. Each morning I would happily go off to school but disappear to the rowing club or the docks instead. Not surprisingly I was down the tubes in my first major school exam, for the Intermediate Certificate.

Even though I had got awful marks I never considered myself stupid, but the headmaster did. When I presented myself the following year in the honours mathematics class he told me to leave: 'Get out of the class, you don't have the intelligence, you'll hold other boys back,' he said. Contrary as ever, and with pure determination, I caught up and finished top of the class with honours.

The same headmaster, and he was a good man, expelled me one time towards the end for causing a strike and creating a rumpus. Subsequently, with a bunch of other lads, happily expelled, I stood outside the railings when the headmaster came out and looked me in the eye with rage.

'Report to my office right away, young man,' said he through the iron railings.

'I will not,' I replied defiantly, which rendered him almost speechless, as his fair complexion turned peach red.

'Why not?'

'You've expelled me; I'm outside the school grounds and outside your jurisdiction.'

So my formal schooling ended slightly prematurely though there was only a short time to go before the final examinations. However, in fairness to the Jesuits and my teachers, they were very good and tolerant, and I was allowed to return to school to sit my Leaving Certificate examination.

It was only squares, swots and grade hunters that read books as far as I was concerned. Being a pragmatic individual I much preferred to be out and about, taking things apart and fixing them or—perhaps closer to the truth—breaking things. One time, for example, I woke up to the fact that I'd never accidentally broken a window. To break some on purpose would, I figured, be much more fun; so I organized a bunch of lads and we made a night of it . . . that was before I found a better outlet for my energies.

The one exception to my contempt for reading in my youth was books of the sea. One story which had a deep influence on me was Joshua Slocum's voyage alone around the world in his yacht *Spray*. Slocum's fascinating account in a simple style of his voyage in a relatively old, inexpensive boat really captured my imagination. He cut out a lot of the baloney and got straight on to the story of *Spray*. In particular I remember how he voyaged through the Straits of Magellan rather than round Cape Horn. One night he was anchored and concerned about wild Indians attacking him while asleep, so he scattered thumb tacks on the decks, which worked a treat when the barefooted Indians sneaked on board.

Having finished school, the time had come to face the rigours of the real world. I didn't. Instead I went to university in Galway to study engineering, though later I switched to economics and commerce because I preferred the 'crowd'. Unlike school I thrived in the liberal academic world of college. There was no discipline to rebel against.

Within months we had formed a sailing club, complete with a grant from the college authorities. I did a lot of sailing and occasionally some work.

Busy as a bee, there was little that I was not involved in from chess to student politics; in short, O'Coineen had a finger in every pie. In other ways I was a loner, combining a massively extrovert personality with a very introverted side. I was accused of being lucky—with raffles, exams and such things—but maybe this was because I would try or chance anything. A chancer you might say. If you're not in you can't win, and you'll never find out unless you try—that was my simple philosophy.

As a long-haired, freaky student, I joined the mountaineering club and went off climbing on Sundays in beautiful Connemara. Whether it was climbing or swimming or running, I always took a somewhat perverted delight in pushing myself to the limits of endurance.

One of my few claims to fame at that time was coming third in the college pub-crawl competition. This was an annual affair held during College Rag Week for charity. It is regarded by many as a prestigious event, the winners of which are pointed out to strangers with awe. 'That's the fella; he must have a stomach like a mop and a helluva plumbing system.'

Not surprisingly, the prize for the winning team is a barrel of beer, and everyone cheats as much as they can get away with. Each team carries its drinker (yours truly) on a stretcher and he may neither run nor puke, under pain of disqualification. It's three miles and seven pubs round the heart of Galway, with a full pint at each. For all the crowds and tension at the start it might be the Olympics—and indeed the event is the culmination of days and hours of training, first with water and then with beer, to extend your capacity. In my case, knocking pints of the old H_2O back rapidly was an economy measure.

Cute as bedamn, I had arranged an airbed on my stretcher—it is the bumping that really knackers the drinkers, and I thought it would absorb the shocks. After a short cut unnoticed by officials, we were up in the lead and, roaring and shouting, urging the bearers on, I was rapidly losing count of those great pints, lined up ready for us at each bar. In the end the bouncing took effect and I brought up discreetly (so that the judges wouldn't see) in a telephone box, but I roared home to glory.

Another time during Rag Week there was a boatless boat race down the old canal which naturally I won, being of a fiercely competitive nature. The competition included a Mini car lashed to big barrels, and a man desperately keeping above water by means of 150 balloons which burst one by one as the race proceeded. Having established an early reputation as an expert in boating affairs, my pride was at stake. My secret weapon consisted of two plastic drain pipes, a pair of pyjamas for stream-lined effect and a car seat lashed on top powered by one Mp (Man power) using canoe paddles. Good training for the North Atlantic, I wonder?

In no time the unreal student days were gone. Once again, it was time to face the so-called reality of the commercial world. To follow the route of my friends in accountancy or office work offered no charms at all. Travel—a form of escape—was what I wanted. There were few opportunities and no money for such luxuries but somehow, anyhow, I must postpone the inevitable settling down into the fur-lined mousetrap. Only in insecurity and travel could I find the stimulation I wanted. Westward, chasing the sun as it set beyond the sea horizon, I should come— as Columbus discovered—to a neighbouring continent.

2

An Idea is born

AS A YOUNG emigrant to the great new world of the Americas, Cormac O'Coineen would almost certainly have stepped ashore on Staten Island, New York, before it was overlooked by the Statue of Liberty. His great-great-grandson arrived here as a twenty-year-old on 3 July 1976, on the 53ft ketch *Creidne*, named after a sea-goddess from Celtic mythology. We had come as the official representatives from Ireland to celebrate America's two hundredth birthday. The United States is a country which boasts forty million people of Irish extraction. A thousand of them now stood, less than a hundred yards away, on-shore at Liberty Wharf: a thousand and more flag-waving Irish Americans, complete with a pipe band and a rostrum full of politicians and dignitaries, waited to greet us. Quite understandably, the crowd were annoyed at having been kept waiting in the hot sun for over an hour for us to get this far, but it was difficult to keep a straight face.

Though but a ketch, the *Creidne* had been selected among the first to lead the massive fleet of tall ships in a spectacular display of sail up the Hudson River the following day, Independence Day.

The *Creidne,* skippered by an old friend, Captain Healy, had instructions to arrive at Liberty Wharf by noon, on 3 July . We were to be the first foreign vessel to land at this recently renovated slum area on the New Jersey shore, and although some of us, myself included, had picked up some notions of celestial navigation and the use of the sextant on the voyage over, none of this helped in this final hundred yards—Liberty Wharf had last been used as a naval base during World War II, and the charts were totally out of date.

Being a man of caution and an excellent navigator, the Skipper had us in the area with plenty of time on hand. The sailing instructions had simply stated, 'Liberty Wharf on the Jersey shore behind the Statue of Liberty'. A launch, which was to meet us to lead the way in, did not show up.

'What will we do, hmmm . . .? You see our dilemma, you agree with me, you see the problem,' Skipper muttered as he walked the decks.

Time was slipping by. It was hot and humid. Skipper searched the area cautiously for the elusive wharf with an understandable fear of running aground. We could hear and see the crowd in the distance. Frustration and tension started to mount. Americans do not like to be kept waiting, and they were not to know what was keeping us.

Eventually a Coast Guard launch came to our assistance. They too had confessed ignorance of the locality, as they had been drafted down from Long Island to help control the great influx of boats for fourth of July celebrations. With the aid of a lead-line to check depth, the Coast Guard crew nonetheless found the way in.

At last the assembled crowd and the TV cameras focused as we majestically followed the launch and came into full view. The cheering grew louder, the pipe band blasted Irish reels . . . Not a hundred yards to go. The atmosphere was delirious.

Then came a thump. The Coast Guard launch forged ahead, but not the *Creidne—Creidne* was stuck fast in the mud on the dropping tide. The launch turned back to pull us off, but we would not budge. Silence fell on the crowd, now approaching the three thousand mark, then laughter prevailed. There was nothing to be done except to wait for the tide to refloat us.

'Leave the ship right away, take the launch ashore and let the reception begin,' were the orders from the Irish government minister and civil servants ashore.

'I'll do no such thing. A captain must not desert his ship,' was Skipper's reply.

There was a stalemate. The politicians on the rostrum were anxious to get on with their speeches, they could not pass up the opportunity to speak in front of the television cameras and help secure their Irish American vote. The Irish government minister was especially anxious to get on with his prepared speech, which was a request to Irish Americans not to send guns and money to the IRA. (A bomb-scare at his hotel added point to his message.)

Finally it was decided that half of the *Creidne's* crew would go ashore for the reception so that the festivities and speeches could commence. Fortunately I was selected as one of the shore party. The pipe band got going again, the crowd cheered, we were welcomed as heroes and presented with a great big golden key—the key to the city of New Jersey, I was told—by the Mayor.

Heavies from the security police kept the crowds under control as we were flatteringly chased by autograph hunters and young girls. It was indeed a novel way to arrive in America. The public and the crowd wanted heroes and we fitted that bill for America's birthday. Two big bullet-proof limousines whisked us off to a formal dinner, attended by over a thousand people—where there were more speeches and we were presented with medals, for having, like the U.S. wartime servicemen, braved the North Atlantic. The next day, July 4th, the *Creidne* was refloated, inspected by divers, declared safe, and we sailed on up the Hudson.

While the *Creidne* was open to the public, tied up alongside in Manhattan, thousands of curious New Yorkers came on board. Tired of telling the same old story about how we came, our imaginations started to take over somewhat. One evening I overheard a crewman explaining carefully to a native New Yorker how we got our boat (comparatively tiny relative to the other tall ships) across the Atlantic:

'Ya see it's like this. The navy constructed a great big cradle on which we floated the *Creidne*. Then with special international co-operation from both sides of the Atlantic for America's birthday, an Air-Force helicopter lifted it out of the water. Then after a link-up with a jet she was dropped off outside Long Island . . .'

To our utter amazement, this guy actually believed the yarn. A product of generations of big city living, we supposed. With so many amazing achievements to read about in the papers everyday in the U.S., people are now prepared to believe that anything is possible. Maybe they're right.

After rather too many adventures in New York (not the best city for a rest cure), I moved on to Newport, Rhode Island. I wanted to be near boats, learn all I could, and get a job on a yacht going south for the winter. With my cousin and fellow crewman Brian, I taught sailing at the local school and worked as a waiter at night.

The restaurant specialized in seafood, and one day a big fat, noisy and arrogant man from the Mid-West came in for a meal. It was seemingly his first visit to the sea and his first dish of fresh lobster.

Having seen the original off-green lobster, the man simply could not understand how it had changed colour: the lobster, complete with all the paraphernalia to dress it up, was a bright red. 'Hey, you goddam Irish waiter, what have you done to my lobster!' the man roared.

We simply laughed. The madder he got, the more we laughed and said: 'Begob, if you were left sitting in a boiling pot you'd soon change colour.' Furious to see us laughing at him, the man turned the colour of the lobster.

As the season ended, I was fired—just as well, for I had found a berth on a 48ft ocean-racing yacht heading south towards warmer waters.

'Where are you bound?' I had asked the skipper one day on the Newport marina.

'Annapolis on the Chesapeake and we're short a hand.' That evening I was at sea with four strangers, not even knowing where Annapolis was but going south nonetheless. The yacht came to be my home for the next two months, and I was to learn a great deal about racing under sail. The skipper's wife, some twenty years his junior, was from South Africa and her attitudes about most things ensured that we had great arguments. She must have been brought up to a life of leisure for she was a great screwball. She had a high regard for black South Africans. 'Everybody should have eight or nine of them,' she would say, meaning she liked them in bed.

Her spouse was excellent company. We talked a great deal about ocean passages and in particular survival at sea, liferafts and such equipment. He spoke of a friend who went to inflate his liferaft in an emergency situation but to his utter horror it would not inflate. Sealed up in a canister as it is, you never know how it will function until it's time to use it. Then maybe it's too late—you're history.

Eventually we put in to Annapolis, which I discovered to be a thriving yachting centre as well as a Navy town with very friendly people. Here I landed a job working in a boatyard for Pete Jackson, an honest, fun-loving man recently settled down after a nomadic life. The little hair left on his bronzed head was greying, but his blond moustache and youthful mind was full of spark and vigour. It was he who introduced me to another Irishman and this set a seal on me: Tim Curtis.

Tim Curtis was then the Managing Director of Zodiac of North America, a French inflatable boat company. On our first meeting we talked a great deal about inflatable boats and what they are capable of doing with modern developments in material and design. Likewise we discussed the concept of sailing liferafts and the possibility of developing some designs. As I left Annapolis in November, the possibility emerged that I might go and work for Zodiac.

My new yacht, *Madrine,* a 50ft ketch, was a beautiful cruising craft. I had been taken aboard as part of a delivery crew for the 2,000-mile run down south to St Lucia in the West Indies. (The owner of my previous vessel had swapped the boat for some land in upstate New York with some cash thrown in.)

The first 700 miles to Bermuda were rough—four days out, as we were crossing the Gulf Stream, we tangled with a hurricane. We survived, not much the worse for wear and with few stories to tell other than that the seas were mountainous. Running off before the storm did the trick.

Clear of the storm, we thrashed along in the trade winds past St Martin with scarcely a bother in the world. Out on deck at four in the morning we inhabited a world of stars and salt. As we stood in the gentle tropical breeze I told my crewmate Al of my plan to cross the Atlantic in a rubber dinghy.

'You're thinking of crossing the Atlantic in an inflatable boat! . . . As an interesting experiment? . . . You must be out of your cotton pickin' mind.' (Al came from Mississippi.)

'That's right,' I replied, and went on to develop my ideas on survival at sea, the sheer adventure and challenge of it all.

'I'll bet you'd never have the guts to do anything like that,' Al said abruptly, 'You're just talking.'

'Why not?' said I, somewhat taken aback by the suggestion that I lacked guts and, though we never got down to talking money for the bet, the notion of such a venture was born there and then.

3

Preparing for the Atlantic

FROM THAT starry night and following visits to several West Indian islands, surviving on sun, sea, bananas and pineapples, my mind was made up. Come hell or high water, O'Coineen was going to cross the Atlantic by inflatable boat. I developed a stubborn determination to see it through, but how? There was a new sense of purpose, but there wasn't a great deal else. For my parents and family it would be a surprise homecoming of their prodigal son. I would leave America quietly, land unnoticed on the beach at Kilronan, Aran Islands, off the west coast of Ireland. Then I'd stroll up to the American Bar for a pint of Guinness, and give my mother a call to say that I was home.

Ignorance is bliss. Had I known the fear, the setbacks and unseen dangers ahead, would I have gone? Even from the deck of a 50ft ketch it was an eerie, unforgettable sight, those merciless gigantic waves, of 30 feet and more, following each other and crashing down, each one seemingly bigger than the last. The horizon like a moving mountain range with spray flying, and howling wind in all directions. Then that feeling down at the bottom, between the waves and walls of surging water.

The West Indies island of Barbados was perhaps an odd place to start, but it was here that the U.S. Embassy was located and, before anything else, I had to get back to the States to earn money and start preparations, and to get back into the U.S. I needed a visa. The most common kind was a visitor's visa, but you needed over $1,000 and a ticket home to get one. The authorities had to satisfy themselves that you had no intention of working there in the States. I had every intention of working there and the ticket home would be an expensive one-off affair.

As luck would have it, I found a way around this regulation:

a businessman's visa. In Barbados a borrowed suit, clean shirt and tie and a self-confident manner did the trick.

By contrast, staying in Barbados in a sort of hippy commune, I was virtually broke. Fortunately Tim Curtis of Zodiac sent down a 'plane ticket from Annapolis. The prospect of working for Zodiac was real and I saw this as a way to achieve the ultimate objective.

On the way to Miami Beach for the Boat Show a few months later I pressed Tim, as I had done several times before, to have Zodiac loan me an inflatable for my Atlantic crossing. Finally, after flatly rejecting the idea on several occasions, it seemed that he had come around. One more heave:

'Tim, I've been reading every book available on the subject. My planning and preparation will make sure the project succeeds. The costs won't be great, all I need is an inflatable.'

'Enda, there is one book you should read.'

'What book is that?' I replied, feeling sure that he was finally sold on the idea.

'The Bible.' The message was clear, and that conversation ended abruptly.

A week later, though, he agreed to find me a suitable inflatable for the crossing, but warned that it would be totally my own risk. He had no desire to send me to my death.

That was the first major breakthrough. I stayed on in Florida doing odd jobs fixing inflatables, looking after yachts and washing dishes, gathering as much money as I could. The plan was to wait until May before returning to Annapolis and making final preparations. On studying several alternative routes, weather patterns and so forth, it seemed like a good idea to start from Boston, sail to Halifax, Nova Scotia and then St John's, Newfoundland, before making the main Atlantic crossing to the west coast of Ireland. By going this way I would have the prevailing winds from the west behind me the whole way.

I based myself in Fort Lauderdale and stayed on board a 60ft yacht at Harbour West marina in return for caretaking. For $400 I also bought my first car, a great big Plymouth station wagon which was christened "Biddy" at the South Port bar with a bottle of Miller beer.

I spent many hours in libraries researching and reading every survival story available, and every bit of information in print

concerning seafaring and the North Atlantic. Slowly the fact
came home that very little was known about a voyage such as
this; increasingly it would be left to me to dream up ways of
achieving the objective.

The next step was to point Biddy in the direction of Annapolis
and go to pick up the promised inflatable. Driving without
insurance or tax, I had to watch out. I'd already got in the way
of an expensive sedan, but when the police arrived to survey the
bent wing, I was miles up the road, spinning along on balding
tyres. If I kept out of a southern jail I had only luck to thank.

'Hey son, do you realize that you've been exceeding the State
of Georgia's speed limits?' the police officer said in his slow
southern drawl after dismounting from his motorcycle with a
gun at the ready. At first I had not seen him.

'No, no, I'm very sorry your honour, I'm very sorry, I didn't
realize . . .' I yattered on, speaking as fast as I could and as if I
had just got off the boat from Ireland and was the most innocent
of twenty-one-year-olds. Most of all I wanted to divert his
attention from the state of the car and asking me about insurance.
I had heard too many stories about nasty Georgia cops throwing
people in jail.

Evidently my accent was so unusual on this back road that
few tourists travel, the police officer was content to give me a
lecture about different laws for drivers in America and Ireland.

Eventually I made a safe arrival at Annapolis with Biddy,
complete with a "new" engine collected from a scrapyard.

'She is over there in the corner,' Tim Curtis pointed out, after
I had spent some minutes trying to find the new inflatable in
the Zodiac warehouse. The boat was by no means new. It was
a rolled-up lump of rubber in the corner. At that time the
inflatable was two years old and it had seen much use.

'It may look a mess but it's in good shape, it's famous already
and has been used in the making of two films—*Airport '77* and
King Kong,' Tim said and pointed to the black UDT across the
back, short for Underwater Demolition Team. Ironically these
were two disaster movies! This gesture must surely have been
by design but no, Tim assured me, it was a complete accident.

Both of these films were shot by MGM on location in many
parts of the world. The boat is the one reputed to have been
gobbled up by King Kong, the monster himself. As the 'plane

crash-landed in *Airport' 77,* the inflatable was there to rescue the survivors from the sea, one of these being the movie star, Jack Lemmon.

On first unrolling that black and grey hunk of rubber it seemed that King Kong had taken a big bite out of the wooden transom. In fact the transom had been cut down to take a short-shafted outboard motor and it proved to be a relatively easy job to build it up again, otherwise with a following sea the waves would have washed in faster than they eventually did.

On inflation in the warehouse that hunk of rubber started to look more like a boat and acquire a personality of its own. Of course a boat is one thing but an ocean-going vessel is another, and this is what I had to achieve. Two of the five tubes were losing air and the inflatable keel also had leaks. But these problems could be overcome—and in time they were: it's hard to beat a real incentive, namely, that if I went out on the ocean unprepared, my life would not be worth this piece of paper.

Tim and his family looked after me well, despite the leaky boat. I doubt whether he really believed that I would go through with the project. The fact that I had no money did not help either.

Following the abrupt departure from my previous waiting job in Newport, my style had improved somewhat and I talked my way into a job waiting at the elegant Maryland Inn restaurant. Being close to Washington DC, we got all sorts of important people to feed such as senators and big tycoons. The job suited grand, working by night for readies and by day in preparation for the crossing.

By this time a game plan had emerged. All advice, books read and weather studies indicated that late June, July and August were the best months to make the crossing. Though the ocean is well known for its unpredictability, during the summer over the North Atlantic you can expect the winds to be either from the north-west, south-west or west for eighty per cent of the time.

'I'll buy you a seat home on a Jumbo instead, you silly boy,' was the reaction of Bill Hutchings who ran the local chandler's called Fawcett's, when I first asked him for help with chandlery and discounts. By this stage I was getting hardened to being treated as a bit of a madman, but when he saw how determined

I was, Bill came round and kindly helped.

Advice flowed fast and free. It came in curious ways. One gentleman offered to contribute a gun for shooting sharks en route, while another offered to paint his company's name on the bottom of the boat and pay for the advertisement.

'And how are you going to power the rubber duck across the ocean?' a naval architect asked.

'At best you'll only be able to take enough fuel to motor for a few hundred miles—and that's if your motor doesn't break down first,' added his partner.

Clearly some sort of sailing rig was needed. A castaway trying to survive after being shipwrecked would need a simple yet efficient rig, so simplicity and the ultimate interpretation of Murphy's law ranked foremost in my thinking.

'And what in God's name is Murphy's Law?' asked the naval architect, his red whiskers bristling. Clearly Murphy had not much of a bearing on his career as a naval architect.

'Murphy,' I explained, 'was a famous Irish engineer whose basic law states that what can go wrong will go wrong.'

'Check! But what has that got to do with rig design?'

'Everything: the next step from that basic law is that the less you have to go wrong, the less you have to go wrong. So I am looking for utter simplicity.'

My friends remained sceptical, but nonetheless proved very helpful. One concept they came up with was brilliant. This involved hanging a sail on a gaff between a tubular tripod which would be mounted on the tubes. It would have had one and a half inch aluminium tubing with a lateen sail. This sail would be lashed onto a long gaff which converted, when needed, into a yard for a squaresail. In the final analysis I concluded that the cost of construction and development would be prohibitive. The mast rig I settled on was a length of alloy tubing with cross supports as a mast, using towing hooks glued to the side for mast support lines. The sail was square and simple; for reaching and sailing upwind it was convertible to a lateen sail with a gaff. On the transom I hung a very clever Finnish invention called the Outboard Sail: on a bracket like that of an outboard motor, I had a sail rigged instead of the engine. All of this, combined with leeboards and plenty of anti-chafe precautions, made for quite an efficient little rig.

The next major piece of equipment was a small motor. Fortunately Tim Curtis had recently sold a batch of inflatables with outboard motors to a group of Arabs who needed them to land armies on beaches; a call to the outboard motor suppliers OMC, and I had a spanking new six h.p. Johnson.

'Hey, give that kid a motor!' was more or less how the conversation went, and it was done.

With time my junk of King Kong rubber developed its own personality and a name emerged: the *Kilcullen,* the name of a great aunt I had in the Virgin Islands; it was also a link with the old family surname and also an association with the Cuculainn, the ancient warriors of Ireland in Celtic mythology.

I began sea trials on Chesapeake Bay and kept adding bits of equipment such as a camping gas stove, a steering compass, a plastic sextant for navigation, and a large water pump which was to prove very useful. By this time I had decided to load the lot into faithful old Biddy, still spluttering on around the roads of Annapolis, and drive to Boston.

Leaving Annapolis was a wrench, for I had made many good friends, and though we all need to be on our own from time to time, good company and friendship is what I value most of all.

A man much more eloquent and pragmatic in regard to the above sentiments than I could ever hope to be, is Tristan Jones. A pure Celt of Welsh origins and born at sea, Tristan happened to sail into Annapolis around this time—quite literally on the back of a truck. His yacht, *Sea Dart,* was also travelling on the back of the truck, together with a supply of his first book *The Incredible Voyage.* This book, together with James Joyce's *Ulysses,* was to be my companion in print on the North Atlantic as I turned my soggy pages while peeling off the sea-miles.

Without having to explain myself or justify the *Kilcullen* plans, Tristan instantly understood and gave good advice. He was a seaman who (as *The Times* put it) handled his pen with the same skill that he handled his boats, and he was to have a significant impact on my life.

It was in New York's Manhattan that Tristan Jones says he learned the true meaning of solitude: 'I who had probably been truly alone more than anyone else on earth—for fifteen months during my Arctic voyage in *Cresswell,* 20 years ago . . . It was in New York that I encountered very real solitude . . . It was here that I learned that true loneliness and boredom are only possible in a crowd.' He then went on to say that solitude—not loneliness—is a wonderful thing, as I was to discover.

Back at Annapolis in Marmaduke's Public House a going-away party was hosted for me and then I was on my way, alone but complete with Biddy—her tyres smoother than ever, a spluttering engine—and *Kilcullen*. Driving through New York was a terrifying experience; for a time afraid to slow down on the great twelve-lane highways and then lost in the vast impersonal concrete jungle which seemed to stretch on forever.

But New York, where one could feel so lonely, was left behind and the next week, having unpacked everything in the snug harbour of Marblehead outside Boston, I perched in the corner pew of a crowded church on a Sunday morning alone with my thoughts and God. It was July 16th and below in the harbour, the *Kilcullen* was berthed alongside, ready for the Atlantic—or so I thought.

4

Alone at last

WHEN I HAD said goodbye to my friends who had come
down to see me off, I could find no further excuse to delay, and
the *Kilcullen* and I cast off from the quayside. Well blessed with
a full stomach, and with the warm summer sun glistening off
the water, I dipped the *Kilcullen*'s oars, though it seemed criminal
to disturb the tranquil sea. Externally I appeared confident but
deep down I felt a sort of trembling fear. A strange quiet had
descended on the quayside as I pulled away. It seemed as if the
whole world was watching.

'You're not of consequence, it's a case of mind over matter:
you don't matter and the world doesn't really mind,' I mused.
A friendly voice broke in on my meditations: 'Will you accept
a tow out of the harbour?' 'No way, only over my dead body,'
I replied in a determined manner. 'It will be my own steam the
whole way.'

This was all very well in theory. Psychologically I was prepared
for rowing but not physically. Within half an hour blisters were
starting to emerge. All that fitness training and running during
preparations could not have prepared my hands. The sea is never
to be trifled with. The calm was misleading. Ahead lay 3,000
miles of North Atlantic ocean, the only certain thing about its
weather being, as I've said, its total unpredictability.

'Where are you goin' in that thing? a man called from a
moored yacht as the *Kilcullen* passed.

'To Outer Mongolia . . . but I'm stopping at Ireland on the
way'.

The inflatable did indeed look out of the ordinary. She was
a striking contrast to the neat modern plastic yachts moored in
the harbour. Clumsy she may have looked, but this was the end

product of many months of hard thinking, careful planning, preparation, scraping and scrounging. As I pulled stroke by stroke, out to the deep ocean, her assortment of supplies—water containers, spare rudder, leeboards and so forth—were indeed a sight for confused eyes. Complete with pots and pans, the *Kilcullen* was like a cross between a Boy-Scout camp and a gypsy caravan.

Once I was clear of harbour a nice wind filled in from the south and I began setting sail. This was a slow and cumbersome process but I had all the time in the world. The sails had to be adjusted to balance with the leeboard by trial and error. Anyway, it was not like a dinghy race: I could well be as much as one week on the same tack. The sailing rig balanced the boat very well with the mizzen sail acting as a form of self-steering gear. Most of the time I found that when I had got all the adjustments correct, the tiller could be lashed to the boat herself.

Two small boats had come a few miles out to sea escorting the *Kilcullen*, one being my friend with his inflatable Zodiac, who had offered me a tow, the other being a Pleon Sailing Club of Marblehead rescue boat with a bunch of kids I had made friends with. One young girl was actually crying.

Soon the land moved away and it was time for the escort to turn back to harbour. These craft were not much smaller than the *Kilcullen*.

'So long, Enda, and steer around the rocks,' someone shouted above the noise of the engines. I had always been told that the basic secret of good navigation was to steer around the rocks, and fortunately there are not many rocks in the North Atlantic— or so I thought.

After all the excitement and emotion of departure I was suddenly alone—and aware as never before of just what I had let myself in for.

The Massachusetts coastline blurred in the distance as evening came on and the *Kilcullen* put ever more sea room between her and the land which dropped below the horizon. With the approach of darkness, it was as well to get a good offing and stand a better chance of not being run down.

The sea was a dark plain now, and as I gazed over it, some lines of verse kept going round in my head:

"Where lies the land to which the ship would go?
Far, far ahead is all her seamen know.
And where the land she travels from? Away
Far, far behind, is all that they can say."

The setting sun shot a path of red-gold across the water. On her compass course the *Kilcullen*'s bow pointed due east, a bearing south of Cape Sable on the Nova Scotia coastline, and clear of land on a Great-Circle route; this was my direct line to Ireland.

It was going to be fresh food the whole way—that is fresh from the can. And it was with great difficulty and much searching under the bow that I located the can-opener. Appropriately my first dinner was a can of Irish stew. Into the pot with it. This pot, in turn deposited on a little stove, quickly came to the boil. Mounted on gimbals, the stove was fixed to a wooden box secured to the floorboards and connected directly to a small gas cylinder. Topped up with sweet biscuits the stew tasted as good as any gourmet dinner as I ate the lot straight from the pot. After the meal the pot was rinsed out with sea water; say what you will, at least there would never be any shortage of water for washing up. I then poured fresh water into the same pot and boiled it up to give myself a delectable cup of tea. This rounded off the meal in style, leaving the stomach content.

It was fortunate that the sea remained calm. On board, space was at a premium and bits of gear were scattered all over the place. I spent a long time sorting it all out, if only so I could stretch out for a sleep.

It was now total darkness without even a single solitary star in the sky. The light wind dropped, leaving the sails hanging loose. The night air was warm and close. I was still nervous about being run down by passing ships on account of being so low down—even with a navigation light. This light was hoisted on top of the short mast and, known as a strobe light, produced quick white flashes powered by a six-volt dry battery. With the radar reflector it was the *Kilcullen*'s only protection. The radar reflector had cost about five pounds; hanging from the backstay which ran from the top of the mast to the transom, all it consisted of were two cardboard discs with special reflective material. The theory was that the cardboard discs, mounted at right angles,

reflected back the ships' radar signals so I'd be pinpointed on
their screens. That was the theory: how it would work was
another matter.

> I've been a wild rover for many a year.
> I've spent all my money on whiskey and beer.
> But now I'm returning with gold in great store,
> And I never will be the wild rover no more.

To my heart's content I sang the evening away before inflating
the *Kilcullen's* air-bed. And, in what perhaps might be the ultimate
nuance of civilization at sea, I stripped off naked and slipped into
my new pair of flowery silk pyjamas. Then it was time to brush
teeth and attend to personal toilet. To answer the call of nature
I laid a large number for the bucket which proved a little small
for the job. Never mind—bucket and chuck it, as on even better
appointed yachts. Whatever about pollution, there was plenty
of ocean to absorb O'Coineen's droppings—the great solution
to pollution of course being dilution.

I was startled. Swiftly I realized that I was not alone with the
sea. A swishing noise and the sound of breaking water disturbed
the still night. My heart jumped and I froze solid with fear.
This far out at sea it could only be some shark, that had taken
my left-overs and must now be looking for more. Then there
was a thud and scraping sound on the bottom of the boat. I
thought of whales tipping over yachts in a playful moment.
Then there was silence and nothing could be seen in the blackness.
Whatever it was, it had gone.

After some time I relaxed and crawled into the warm, snug
sleeping bag on the air-bed. Just my head and shoulders lay
uncovered under the open sky. By this time some stars had
appeared on all sides and I stared vacantly at them. Everything
hung loose, rolling about in the gentle swell. It would be a calm
night.

'This is the moment you've worked for. You're going to do
it, there is no stopping you now,' I said to myself, unable to
sleep under the stars but quite content on this little world of air
on the ocean.

The sky grew dark and suddenly, at around midnight, it began
to thunder. In a matter of thirty minutes the sea went from calm

to storm, and good-bye to my new found sense of security. Lightning flashes lit the sky at intervals. The forked tongues seemed to dive down in every direction. The roaring thunder got louder and closer to the flashes as the storm centre approached. The whole world seemed to be shaking and I became very frightened. What would the storm centre bring? A big wave? I did not know. I'd met storms at sea before, but never all on my own in a rubber boat.

It was almost possible to read a book by the light of the lightning flashes. Then the rain came thundering down, penetrating everywhere. The canopy, which I had not rigged up properly in anticipation of the storm, offered little protection. The whole world became one miserable place, the rain water was cold and I huddled to conserve energy as the winds roared above.

Fortunately because the wind came so quickly the seas did not get a chance to build. However the mizzen sail lashings worked loose in a vicious squall. The sail started to flap fiercely and, if left unattended, would have been reduced to shreds in no time. The lightning persisted and, at first with a strong fear of being electrocuted and knowing little about lightning, I was afraid to get up and relash the sail. Eventually I summoned up the courage between flashes, though by then the sail was already in a bad way.

A lone object, a pimple on the surface of the deep, with nothing for miles around to attract attention on the ocean, I felt that this vicious thunderstorm was out to get me personally. Within three hours it was gone. I realized that this cruel, beautiful sea can be very cold and indifferent. One moment it's out to get you with all the fury on earth, and the next, it's purring like a placid cat by the fireside.

The worst of the storm was clearly over but it was still dark. I waited, wet and miserable, alone with my thoughts until dawn. It is said that insecurity can be stimulating and makes one think the unthinkable. Well I did plenty of thinking that night as I didn't feel like trying to sleep. I hoped that the coming day would bring a warm sun and good drying weather, and meanwhile ruminated in the dark on what I was doing here. The next day was indeed fine. By noon nearly everything was put to rights. A rough latitude by sextant put the *Kilcullen* fifty miles from Boston. Progress was slow, averaging two and a half knots, but it was progress nonetheless.

Living in such a restricted area needed discipline—never my strongest point. Virtually every movement had to be carefully worked out for fear of losing gear or being washed overboard.

'You'll have to wear a harness all the time,' I was warned before departure. 'A single-handed sailor without a harness is like a parachutist without a parachute. The only difference is, your death will be a lot slower when you fall overboard.' With nobody on board to come back and pick you up, it would indeed be a slow, miserable death. My adviser was not content with words: he gave me a safety harness in addition to an excellent first-aid kit, and both were very welcome.

Toilet paper, books, biscuits and navigation charts, to mention but a few objects, were all stored carefully in plastic bags, but still the dampness and seawater found their way through. The bow was the driest part but, with so much to store, there was little space for anything and, whenever I went looking for something in particular, virtually everything had to come out. That was normally the time when, with everything exposed, a big wave would come crashing in. It was hopeless trying to stay dry when the wind piped up.

The evening of the second day a coastal steamer chugged past; the *Kilcullen* had obviously caught its attention. The captain stood on the bridge and the crew lined the decks, about five in all; they must have been straining their eyeballs, wondering if I was a rather laid-back castaway.

'Ahoy there, where're ya bound? Is that thing safe?' the captain called out. The ship's name was the *Bell of Hope*. I felt nervous talking with the captain: it was as if the ship was intruding on my privacy. Ashore I had spent long enough trying to explain this voyage, and I had no desire to start again. I felt a bit as though somebody was staring in through my windows when I had no curtains to pull.

'Canada and then Ireland. Where're you bound?'

'Boston. Are you sure you're OK? That sure was a real bad thunderstorm last night. Can we help you in any way? Would you like us to report your position?'

'No, I'm fine, very kind of you to offer, really I'm fine and don't wish to cause any worry.' With that we parted. I was happy to be clear of the *Bell of Hope*. I did very much appreciate the captain's gesture in altering course and offering help. I had read so many accounts of genuine castaways vainly trying to attract the attention of ships which passed within a mile or less of them to march away over the horizon unheeding. I for one was determined not to be rescued, least of all so early on in my voyage. Anyway, to judge by the crew's reaction behind the captain's straight and courteous face, the sight of the *Kilcullen* had given all on board that ship a good laugh, and it's always good to keep people amused.

Slowly the *Bell of Hope* dieappeared over the horizon as the deep chugging of the ship's diesel reverberated in all directions, and her plume of black smoke drifted across the clear evening sky.

While during the day I felt in control, night time was different. With night came fear of the unexpected. I'd be glad to say that I was tough, fearless and brave but if the truth be known, I was terrified out of my wits. Only that strange inner motivation kept its hold on me.

The *Kilcullen's* tubes went soft as the sun went down. This was nothing to be alarmed about; it happened because of the drop in temperature, and I had air bellows to top up the pressure. Air temperature is something one should always be conscious of in an inflatable boat or liferaft. For each degree in temperature change the pressure change is three millibars. By simple feel or by the use of a pressure gauge, it was possible to control this. If the pressure is too low there is a danger that extra chafe will wear a hole in a tube, while in hot sun the higher pressure may cause the tubes to burst unless you release some of that air.

Though the night air was warm enough, the *Kilcullen* was now on the edge of the cold Labrador current and, being so close to the water, I was all too conscious of the water temperature. In short, I was bloody cold and miserable through the night. Gradually my body system was adjusting to the movement of the boat, likewise the mental uncertainty with each wave, the flexing of the boat, and the gushing sound as the stubby bow encountered each wave.

By day three the Canadian radio stations were coming in loud and clear on the transistor radio, it was possible to get an approximate navigational bearing from them. It was hot and there was little wind. Though fuel supply was limited I got out the six h.p. outboard motor. Motors on boats are useful. In fact the man who invented them must have had a lot of brains. It was a Johnson which worked a treat and was kindly supplied by my Irish friends in Annapolis.

It was noisy and difficult to stay on course with the motor, so every few hours I would stop for a rest. At each stop the silence was almost deafening. It amplified my feelings of solitude and sense of being very much alone, out of sight of land, on this vast watery plain.

My plan was to make Halifax, rest there for a few days and then continue to St. John's, Newfoundland, 500 miles beyond that, and then straight for Europe. As mentioned previously, this is the shortest way across the Atlantic, though on a standard North Atlantic Mercator chart it may not seem this way. However the Great-Circle line goes through New York, Boston, Halifax and St John's—almost. This all seemed totally logical. The snag was that the *Kilcullen*'s departure was later than it should have been. With the winter coming sooner the further north, a northern route carried with it a greater risk of meeting strong winds, fog, and the dreaded icebergs. For good measure the delay would also mean being at sea in September, a time of vicious equinoctial gales.

Cold was also a problem and the *Kilcullen,* over this route, would have to sail the Labrador current for the first third of the journey at least before picking up the Gulf Stream. I'd considered all this before setting out, but as I sat now puttering slowly under engine towards Halifax, I was inclined to rethink my strategy from scratch.

Now over four days out, the *Kilcullen* was eighty miles west of Cape Sable—I had what seemed to me a good celestial fix, accurate to about fifteen miles. Cape Sable, on the southern tip of Nova Scotia, had strong contrary tides and was often shrouded in eerie fog. It was usually bad news for mariners.

But I'd not yet reached Cape Sable, and felt confident and in control. 'Yippee, yahoo, whee . . .' I roared and shouted into the gathering night. There was nobody to hear, be upset, or to comment about my rantings and ravings, so why worry?

The night remained calm. The magnificent stars—the Plough, Orion and many beautiful constellations had once again made their reappearance. With sails hanging loose my night passed comfortably under the canvas cover. The moon, in its three-quarter state, was bright and clear as I attempted to identify the small pot holes, or craters on its surface. Every now and then the inflatable moved slightly on the gentle swell, as I listened to the Canadian Top Twenty before dropping off to sleep.

I awoke with a start and crawled frantically out of the snug sleeping bag under the canvas cover. There was a deep pounding and rumbling sound, the screech of seagulls and an awful smell of fish.

On peering up from the cover I saw a deep-sea trawler towering over me; the noise was coming from its diesel motors slowly ticking over. Curious faces peered down. No words seemed appropriate—besides, I was startled to wake up to the sight of these fishermen.

Finally I greeted them, feeling much the same as I did during the previous encounter with the *Bell of Hope*. But first I found the flag halliard and hoisted the Irish tricolour.

'Good morning, nice weather we're having, isn't it?' Dawn had broken and the day did indeed look promising.

'Nice weather indeed.'

Talking about the weather does break the ice, whether at the local pub or sitting in a rubber boat somewhere off Canada. It gives both parties a chance to size each other up before making a more debatable statement.

'Can you give me a position fix?' I went on.

'You're sixty miles due west of Sable. Where you from lad, and where are ya bound?' a voice replied, evidently the captain's. Once again, like with the *Bell of Hope* I felt threatened and having to explain myself. Rather than say Ireland, it seemed easier to say Halifax.

'Do you realize how far Halifax is?' a crewman called out.

'I do.'

'Where have you come from in that thing?' another queried

'Boston,' I replied proudly, already feeling a strong sense of achievement at having come this far.

'You must be crackers! Are you sure you're safe?'

'I would feel safer on board this boat riding out a storm than on yours—Sir.' I added Sir, not wishing to sound too cheeky.

There was a silence then:

'You must be a young wee bit of an adventurer, the sort we

read about in books . . . You crackers boy, but fair play anyhow.'

I missed the name of the trawler but it was from Yarmouth on the Nova Scotian coast. We parted company as the fishermen went about their business. Again the *Kilcullen* powered along under motor in the flat calm. By going flat out at four and a half knots I expected to round the Cape by midnight. True, navigation charts and Sailing Directions all warn of strong tides in this area and to stay well clear of this rugged and often dangerous coastline, prone as it was to fog. What I did not have for this area were tide tables—now I dearly wished I'd had them to sort out some calculations.

All afternoon I watched out for land. Visibility was good, but, as the saying goes, a watched pot never boils. A steady wind carried us along and progress was good. By evening before the fog set in a series of small specks emerged on the horizon which turned out to be a fleet of fishing boats. Then everything disappeared in the fog and the night.

The *Kilcullen* and her captain sailed blindly on. It was nerve-racking, though maybe I should have been more worried. The bow was hardly visible from the stern, and I had to rely totally on the compass as I crouched with the tiller under my armpit—fearing on the one hand to be caught up in the fierce tidal race, while on the other hand I did not want to sail too far out to sea. The latter option being the lesser risk, I steered a south-easterly course: this would ensure a wide berth of the Cape, and after about nine hours it would be possible to alter course for Halifax with safety.

It was cold. My hands were frozen on the tiller. Despite three layers of clothes and oilskins the cold still found its way in. This extreme temperature was such a marked contrast to the warm sun of six hours previously. Still the fog persisted. This is, apparently, an almost permanent feature of this coastline. It is caused by the icy waters of the Labrador current meeting the warm landmass. During the summer, the land of course heats up much quicker than the sea, causing an enormous difference in temperature. Once you are thirty miles or more away from the coast, out to sea, the fog gradually disappears. I longed to be miles out to sea, way off on the Atlantic but struggled on through the cold. There was no alternative.

Unwittingly the *Kilcullen* sailed through a large fishing fleet.

At first I thought the trawler lights meant a lighthouse and land, but no, I nearly ended up caught in some nets! Besides the potential mess and danger, the prospect of having to explain the voyage again—they might have insisted on rescuing me in the darkness—did not appeal to me. A position fix would have been welcome but on balance I preferred to give all other craft a wide berth.

Suddenly I was out of the fog. The loom of a lighthouse appeared on the horizon ahead but the next moment I'd vanished into another bank of cotton-wool fog and quite lost the light. A radio direction finder would have been useful, as would a VHF radio transmitter to check position, however these were items that I could not afford. Besides, with such limited space, storage would have been a problem and it would have been virtually impossible to keep them dry.

By this time I was starting to feel exhausted. A heavy swell was running as the wind increased. The prospect of being shipwrecked on this rugged shoreline was frightening. I started to visualize the *Kilcullen* being torn to shreds on the sharp rocks, and trying desperately to hold on before being swept away to a watery grave.

Being lost this way, I had always imagined, would be a horrible way to die. All alone, away from friends and family. I started to pray. Up until now the *Kilcullen* had been very lucky but would that luck hold? Only time would tell.

The night passed slowly. It was lonely and wretched, not knowing what the next moment would bring. The hours slipped past as the *Kilcullen* sailed blindly on. I couldn't make a decision: was it time to alter course for land? Had I cleared the Cape? Was I running too far out to sea? Eventually confidence returned and I firmly altered course to make directly for Halifax.

The wind persisted but the sea swell disappeared. Strange, I thought, perhaps it was the effect of the land after rounding the Cape. The *Kilcullen* was well out to sea. Not to worry, everything was quite safe. Though the fog was as thick as ever it had started to get bright and warm up a little, which made me relax, secure in the knowledge that the dreaded Cape Sable had finally been beaten.

Suddenly there was a swishing sound, a running through seaweed followed by a gentle thud and the bold ship *Kilcullen* came to an abrupt halt. I hadn't seen a thing.

Where in God's name was I? There was no doubt that we were aground. The whole thing seemed absurd. After days of dead-reckoning and so-called careful navigation, here I was lost and aground, having run straight into Canada for my first visit without even seeing it! Nothing could be seen in any direction. What next? Would the *Kilcullen* be torn up on the rocks? How would I get out of this one?

5

Steering around the rocks

WHAT NOW? This must surely be some part of Canada that the *Kilcullen* has hit, but where? Aground and lost. The situation had its funny side, but I was not in a mood to appreciate it. At least there was one advantage in single handed sailing: there was no one else to mock me for my bad navigation.

For about half an hour the fog lifted slightly. There were outlines of land all around. Fortunately it was gentle beach we had run up on, having just missed a reef by pure chance on the way in. I got afloat again with a determination to get safely back out to sea as soon as possible, but I kept hitting land. Then the fog closed in again, but not before I had found a landing jetty—it towered some thirty feet above my head, which shows how much the tide had dropped. It must surely have been this massive tide range that had swept the *Kilcullen* off course.

It was strange to be back on solid land and with my sea-legs under me, I walked in a drunken manner. There was a small shack which contained old tools, ropes, petrol and parts of an outboard motor. I was afraid to go far from this shack for fear of getting lost in the fog, but then I stumbled upon a path with guiding sticks.

This led to a two-storey house beyond a lighthouse which loomed up out of the ground. Layered in fog, there was great mystery about the place. I had visions of some dumb lighthouse keeper chasing me away with a shotgun, in case I was trying to rob him. In a place as remote as this, miles from anywhere, living an isolated life, a man was bound to be very suspicious of strangers.

It was about 6.30 in the morning as I reached the house. There was a light on in one of the rooms. Nervously I waited outside summoning up enough courage to knock on the door. When I did knock, it was so feeble that nobody heard. I rapped again more loudly. Still silence. I tried the handle and opened the door. I was looking right into the lighthouse keeper's living-room. A woman sat comfortably in an armchair looking at me. 'Come on in,' she yelled. 'Have a cup of coffee.' I was a bit taken aback. I don't know why—perhaps I expected the whole place to be deserted in this eerie fog. Anyway a moment later I was sitting between Noreen and Albert by a cosy-stove having a hot breakfast and answering their questions about my journey. They treated me like a long-lost son, plying me with food, drink and questions, till I was too sleepy to do anything but start nodding off, when they put me to bed. They made me feel so much at home, I quite changed my mind about vanishing into the fog as I had come, but stayed with them—and their helper, Tim, a boy a little younger than me—until the weather cleared. They waved me good-bye as I set off, an Irish jig playing on my tape-recorder, a bottle of Guinness in hand. Then the gathering darkness swallowed them up, but their friendly light stayed with me far out to sea.

The lighthouse visit was a most curious one. To a visitor the island (Peace's Island) was just a bleak, barren outcrop of rock and weed, but Noreen and Albert loved it in spite of the vicious winter gales and the huge boulders of ice. For some time afterwards I kept up a correspondence with the keepers, but now, they have gone, making way for automation.

I was still some twenty miles the wrong side of Cape Sable. The lights I had seen were those of Yarmouth. Cape Sable was once again a worry and an obstacle. It was a tricky course to plot, with so many islands in the area—I was told that there were 365 of them, adding extra confusion during leap years.

Steering a careful south-easterly compass course, the *Kilcullen* whined along at four knots under motor, as my friends at Peace's Island had even topped up my fuel supply. After four hours, helped by the tide, calculations indicated that we were almost at the Cape; then the tide turned. The following six hours, again in fog, were misery itself. The dampness was horrible as I sat huddled up in the stern, motoring full blast, fighting a battle with the merciless tide. Suddenly land appeared. The cliffs rose up in the air sending shivers down my spine; I was being swept towards them at an alarming rate. I put the *Kilcullen*'s stern to the jagged rocks and punched out against the tide, inching my way seawards.

Would I ever get around this wretched Cape Sable? I mused upon an old square-rigger, *Destiny*, which attempted to round Cape Horn 150 years ago. On a passage from England to Australia, for three solid months her captain and crew were beaten back by one gale after the next as they tried to round the Cape. In the end they were forced to give up, having covered only twenty miles in all that time. Instead the captain turned his ship around to sail two thirds of the way around the world again, to get to Australia, via the Cape of Good Hope.

The day wore on and I persisted blindly. Eventually it was more settled sea conditions and the sight of a passing coastal steamer that convinced me that the Cape had finally been beaten. That journey out of the treacherous fog-ridden tip of Nova Scotia into the open sea was like leaving a dense forest and coming out into green pastures. With full sail set, the *Kilcullen* ran along merrily before the fifteen-knot south-west wind. Next stop, Halifax.

At that stage it became clear that the plan to continue along the coast from Halifax to St John's must be abandoned. At the mercy of coastal fog, the cold and strong on-shore tides, the *Kilcullen* would be difficult to manage. Likewise, with no navigation instruments other than a compass and sextant, which would be fine with sun offshore, my luck could not last. Halifax would now have to be the last stop before jumping for Europe. The ocean passage would be longer, but I'd had enough of coasting.

After the bitter cold of the previous night the sun was warm. I was adjusting more and more to the elements. Each cloud brought something new. The coastline, about twenty miles away, was barely visible—away from land the *Kilcullen* was safe and her skipper happy as the evening approached.

A small speck appeared on the cloudless, clear blue horizon. Curiosity got the better of me and I went towards it. The speck turned out to be a small fishing boat with screeching gulls hovering overhead fighting for discarded fish scraps. The Connemara Ceili band played a lively Irish jig on my little cassette recorder as I put the *Kilcullen* alongside: two astonished fishermen gaped over the bulwarks. A man and a boy.

'Top of the evening to you . . . !' I called out. 'It's a grand sunny one too, isn't it?'

The man and boy looked up in bewilderment from their 18ft open boat, their diesel engine drumming idly—like a solid bass drum beat against the high-pitched screeching of the gulls.

The fishermen's name was Kelly. They were father and son, out of North East Harbour, Nova Scotia. When they had overcome their shyness, we shared a bottle of Guinness and swapped yarns. They had never tasted this famous brew but they had heard about it.

'As a matter of fact,' Kelly said in his high-pitched sing-song voice, 'my father's father came from Cork. He was shipwrecked on a ship carrying salt near Cape Sable. He fell in love with a girl in the family that rescued him and there was hell to play but eventually they got married. He never did go back home again and took to the fishing ever since.'

It seemed so strange chatting away in the warm evening sun, miles from land, as we rolled in the gentle Atlantic swell. Though over two thousand miles of ocean is in the way, the Kellys have a great deal in common with the fishing folk on the west coast of Ireland. They too live a rough, simple and God-fearing life, close to nature and the unforgiving elements. This life was such a contrast to the hectic pace of New York with the constant stress and strain I had known as I fought my way in and out of the subway twice a day.

The contrast was now complete.

Though old man Kelly did not say it, I could see from his wrinkled face that he needed to move on as the evening advanced. He will have taken quite a yarn back with him to the harbour. If ever you visit a pub in North East Harbour and you hear a strange yarn about some wild-haired apparition playing Irish jigs, who appeared out of the blue in a rubber boat, you'll know where the yarn came from.

Night. I dozed off, dreaming of Halifax and the pleasures of civilization—a hot bath and a spring bed. Red sky at morning: the yachtie's warning. Indeed, a dense black mass of cloud slowly accumulated to the south and headed in the *Kilcullen's* direction. The air became sharper and the wind increased. With thirty miles to go, the seas started to build. So close to Halifax and yet so far. Being close to a lee shore in a gale spelt danger. I was tense and nervous. Occasionally a wave would pick up the *Kilcullen* like a surfboard and toss her about as I hung on for dear life, trying to control the rudder. Surfing the waves was exhilarating and frightening.

I approached the land that afternoon in a roaring gale. Not wishing to push mother luck too far, I handed the mizzen, a cumbersome procedure. Without the mizzen the boat did not want to make it around the last headland close to the pounding surf. Even after setting the mizzen again (and almost falling overboard in the process), I couldn't hold the *Kilcullen* on course. We made a little headway but a great deal of leeway, as we edged past the roaring surf. Everything depended on the outboard motor—if that failed now, the sail would never hold us clear of the breakers.

Past the headland, in the lee of Sombrero Island, we entered more sheltered waters. With sails down and the motor for the last mile using the very last of the petrol, I relaxed blissfully in the calm water. A lot—too much—of the calm water was slopping about in the boat, but I'd reached a safe haven as the storm raged outside.

6

Halifax

THE MOMENT I stepped ashore I felt lonely. Unannounced, unexpected, and scruffy in dirty oilskins, I tied up at the first club I came to, which happened to be The Royal Yacht Squadron.

'You're not a member here, sir. Guests must be signed in and we'd rather that you moved on—sir,' I was told by the superior attendant as I went up to find myself a drink. I moved on in disgust.

I found a better welcome from a Greek lady and her pretty daughter at a quayside café where I was served a meal of greasy fish and chips, which tasted like caviare. I barely had enough money to pay for it.

Alone and unexpected in Halifax, and penniless as usual, I didn't know where I was going to lay my head. Happily though, Mother Luck smiled and I chanced upon Bill Buckley, a hardy Nova Scotian sailor whom I'd met in Florida six months previously. He found me a couch in a friend's apartment.

With many sides to his personality Bill, the black sheep of a respectable family, could be tough and aggressive one moment and charm the birds off the branches the next. He had a way with women, and several were crazy about him, not least for his black curly hair and fair complexion. He is a man of emotion and intuition.

After a hot bath, a change into dry clothes, a couple of beers with Bill and a great night's sleep, I was a new man the following morning. It was considered sensible to call at Customs and Immigration to say that I had arrived, having, at that stage, entered the country illegally. On leaving Boston I had not bothered with any formalities with Customs, nor had I any kind of ownership documents or boat registration—again, breaking the law.

'Where's your yacht?' the official asked.

'This is it,' I replied as we stood beside her on the quayside. He had thought that the *Kilcullen* was the tender to the yacht for which I had requested Customs clearance.

By politeness and glib talk I persuaded the official, who was willing to bend the rules just a little, to make an exception and give me a temporary importation form. He stamped my damp passport. Well, we'd made it here from Boston, and the *Kilcullen*'s skipper was not a little proud of the fact.

Stage One was complete. Time was racing on, and I rapidly started final preparations. The northern route was already out of the question and prudence dictated that I should sail a south-easterly course to pick up the Gulf Stream, before heading straight east and north. I should pick up the Gulf Stream 250 miles southeast of Halifax.

Everybody in Halifax was friendly and helpful, though the boatmaster at the club marina was very suspicious of my intentions. With difficulty I persuaded him to lift the *Kilcullen* out of the water on the club crane. I was not a member so he charged me double the normal fee.

Money was becoming a big problem. There was no way I could call home looking for money, so I reluctantly sent a pleading request to Tim Curtis in Annapolis. He kindly sent me a couple of hundred dollars—pennies from heaven.

The *Kilcullen*'s bottom on inspection was fairly clean and there were few signs of wear, despite my antics off Cape Sable and a shark which had apparently scratched his rear end on the bottom. A special Zodiac anti-fouling compound had also checked marine growth. Her bottom formed a sort of 'V' shape made by the inflatable keel which squeezed between the rubber bottom and the floorboards which I lived on. These boards were wedged in between the air tubes, thus giving the inflatable its rigidity.

When the *Kilcullen* was out of the water I deflated her. She looked a sorry sight without air, just a heap of rubber. I made several minor modifications such as re-locating the floor boxes for more comfortable sleeping and creating more storage space.

I acquired another watch for navigation, together with extra batteries and spares for the outboard motor, which I had serviced for $70—a king's ransom for a man of my means. But more help kept coming my way. Bill had a friend with a surplus survival suit—after working on a Canadian oil rig, he was transferring to the Persian Gulf where he'd find it too hot. It passed to me, as did a warm mustang jacket of Bill's. This gear later was to save my life.

For final provisioning I made for the biggest supermarket in the neighbourhood and filled up two trollies. The dehydrated foods I had tried out on the first part of the voyage, though compact in storage, tasted terrible. They used up a great deal of water and were expensive.

The store's assistant manager was a little taken aback when I told him about my venture and asked for a discount.

He looked at the picture I showed him of the *Kilcullen* under sail, then kindly gave a ten per cent discount, which was the best he could do as an assistant manager, he explained. I promised to send him a postcard with a donkey on it from Ireland when I landed.

There were fifty cans of assorted meats, half of which were Irish stew. Ten pounds of raisins, 35 packages of porridge, packets of soup, drinking chocolate, Bovril, tea, coffee and sugar. There were also large assorted quantities of chocolates, sweets and fruit drink mixes together with an assortment of fruit cans to celebrate Sundays, Holy Days of Obligation and special events. I got a bottle of Mateus Rosé wine for arrival at the Gulf Stream, a bottle of champagne to celebrate the half-way mark, and two bottles of whiskey for in between.

These little perks along the way were important to break up the journey into stages. It was almost like the donkey with a carrot held out on a stick in front of his nose. There was also a large supply of salt and vitamin pills, including iron and vitamin C tablets to fight scurvy.

Getting it all on board was a challenge in itself. Packing suitcases would be child's play by comparison. Odds and ends were stashed all over the place, while all cans were labelled and varnished to stop rust. The one consolation was that, as the voyage progressed, supplies would be used up, creating more space in which to live. Working on the basis of half a gallon a day, I loaded forty gallons of water. I had allowed enough food with some to spare, to complete the voyage in fifty days. As it turned out I had far too much water since it has not been unknown for large quantities of rain to fall on the North Atlantic. Along with all of that there was a solar still on board for severe emergencies. This compact little unit could in theory distill a quart of fresh water a day from sea-water, even in overcast conditions.

Twenty-seven gallons of petrol in three rubber containers, the most dangerous cargo of all, completed the load, making the *Kilcullen* very low in the water. The fuel was enough for 150 miles approximately, to help make the Gulf Stream quickly, with the balance for a landfall—wherever that might be.

By Saturday night, July 30th, everything was finally complete. Sunday would be a day of rest and the plan was to get under way bright and early Monday morning.

My shopping completed, I was down to my last dollar. In my last-minute quest to get some sponsorship, word of the voyage reached the ears of a local trader. His interests included a sex shop, and he informed me that he was very promotion-orientated. In return for allowing him to paint the name of his sex shop on the bottom of the *Kilcullen* he offered me $400. He was even willing to throw in a free inflatable lady for the lone captain of the *Kilcullen* to keep him company. The offer needed serious consideration. There are a lot of things a skipper can do with an inflatable lady, especially in a storm at sea, but in the end, as there was barely sleeping room for one person in *Kilcullen,* I decided I could not make space for her.

Back at the apartment, which seemed like a way house for travellers of all descriptions, mostly of a shady nature, it was decided to put on a party for my last night.

In the early hours of the morning with all of us well tanked up, somebody with a friend who ran a Halifax dock-area brothel called for some ladies to entertain the young sailor. Being a tender 21 years of age and brought up in a very genteel Catholic manner, I found the proceedings downright shocking but very funny . . .

Three ladies in make-up and high heels arrived by taxi. They wore fancy clothes, provocative hair styles and carried, believe it or not, red handbags, just as though they had stepped out of the pages of Damon Runyon.

I was at my wit's end, what with worrying about unmentionable diseases and what-have-you. Before I knew where I was the ladies had stripped your humble sailor, taken hold of his private member and dragged him first to the bathroom—to scrub him down—before carrying him to the bedroom. They sort of sucked me in and blew me out in bubbles.

In order dear reader, to protect my reputation, I should like to state that I think this was all disgusting and that the experience was awful. It would be closer to the truth to say that I enjoyed the novelty of it all, though, leaving the moral aspects aside, I genuinely feel sorry for the girls—there must be a cleaner way to earn a living. I felt rather fragile when I woke in the morning— had I been laughing too much?—and was glad of a bad weather forecast which delayed starting for another day. I needed a clear weather break to get myself well out to sea and reach the Gulf Stream.

Tuesday, the apartment seemed to me very comfortable, the town quite snug. There were the usual traffic jams, buses packed with pretty secretaries, office clerks, dustbin men, surgeons, bank managers and salesmen, all converging to start their working day. By contrast I saw myself as the fool heading out into the unknown for no good reason.

After a telephone call home to my parents, alone and unobserved (for Bill Buckley could not be there to see me off) with little ceremony I untied the mooring lines and made for the harbour mouth.

7

Making for the Stream

'THE SEA knows nothing of money or power. She knows only loyalty and audacity and determination and courage and by God, she knows an unthinking, unseeing fool when she encounters one.'

So writes Tristan Jones when he speaks of Cabbages and Kings in his excellent book: *A Star to Steer Her By*. And sure, the great Tristan articulates my crudely developed feelings about the sea.

To some, tearing up money is tempting fate, a crime that does not bear contemplating. Not so for the *Kilcullen*'s skipper; once clear of land, I tore up my last dollar bill and the wind took the bits out over the deep. It was an ocean traveller's token gesture of farewell to our materialistic world.

There was little wind. Three days later, mostly motoring in the cold fog and Labrador current, we had covered 115 miles according to the Walker log streamed from the transom; connected to a spinner on a long line, this log worked a treat. Though using up the limited fuel supply rapidly, the more the *Kilcullen* shortened the distance towards the eastwards–flowing Gulf Stream the better, so it was all in a good cause. I still kept back a supply of fuel for the critical landfall.

As land receded the fog thinned and the sun fought its way through the clouds. The warmth was welcome, and a wind filled in from the south, allowing me to set the sails. Already my clothes were all damp from the salt air and it was a relief to start peeling off the layers. Likewise for the first time the boat was steering herself under sail, well balanced, and I could start to read my first book: *A Short History of Russia,* 500 pages of ballast.

The small thermometer I had showed an increase in the water temperature, which indicated that the Gulf Stream must be near at hand. This is a most remarkable ocean current whose general path is known but which meanders unpredictably as it gets further north and east. Most North Atlantic navigators know it well but it is not as important to them as it was to the *Kilcullen* with our slow speed and openness to the weather. Interestingly, I say 'our' here instead of 'my' because as time progressed I felt less and less alone—there was always somebody else on board.

Before departing Halifax, I got a detailed fix on the Stream's movement as viewed by satellite. The photograph it takes identifies temperature-bands by different colours, so the Stream can be pinpointed in its colours from day to day. Now it was located some three hundred miles south-east of Halifax, and the *Kilcullen's* course was plotted accordingly. Here the Gulf Stream is about sixty miles—one degree—wide and flows east and north at the rate of between one and one and a half knots. This point, the first target of the voyage, was at 40° 40' N., 60° 00' W. I had the thermometer along to measure progress towards the Stream centre: the books say that you have arrived when the thermometer indicates a consistent water temperature at about ten feet depth.

Between the Labrador Current and the Gulf Stream you can get a difference in water temperature of approximately 20° F. And, as you can imagine, where these currents converge there can be buckets of turbulence, thunderstorms and unsettled weather the like of which I had never seen before.

I was told once about a weather ship stopped in calm weather on the western edge of the Gulf Stream off the American coast. The oceanographers on board wanted to plot rates of flow and temperature. At the bow of the ship the water temperature was 72° F. while at the stern, some 300 feet away, the thermometer in the water was registering 48° F!

Be that as it may, once in the Stream, the general flow east would help the *Kilcullen's* progress by about thirty knots in 24 hours, in addition of course to the increased comfort of it all. At the present rate, I reckoned I should need about another two days to make the Stream and, to celebrate the arrival I set aside a special bottle of wine.

It was now the 6th. I could have wished it were a whole month earlier, for the prospect of running into September, and possibly October, at the present rate before an ultimate landfall, was not pleasing. But my delays in Annapolis, Boston and Halifax could not have been avoided.

'And what's for dinner tonight, young man?'

'The very best from the galley, beans and canned stew.'

It was indeed good. The left-overs, along with my droppings of nature in the form of the first decent crap since sailing, also went over the side. I relaxed to the sound of Johann Strauss on cassette tape deck and a cup of tea; the only other life for miles around were a few terns hovering overhead looking for scraps—or so I thought.

Without flipping the tape I let it play out, leaving me with the quiet of the gentle evening swell. Absorbed as I was in the *History of Russia,* the only sounds came from an occasional squeak from a tern, and the clatter of the rigging in the swell. Then there came the sound of deep breathing, I was unaware of it at first, but it gradually built up and sounded like that of a heavy smoker or a man with bronchitis. I left Russia and looked up to see a black fin stationary about 25 yards away, then another, and another; in sudden terror I could no longer count them as they formed a semi-circle round the *Kilcullen*.

Was this the end? I was scared. Not budging an inch I just stood there and froze with an oar clenched between my fists at the ready. Never mind storms and bad weather, this was something entirely different—there would be nothing but a heap of rubber if the *Kilcullen* got ripped apart by the sharks. Several thoughts ran through my mind. A gun: I'd been offered one and light-heartedly refused it. Sure, it would have rusted anyhow—besides for this lot I'd have needed a machine-gun. At all events, with so much of the shark below the water, I'd probably miss and shoot a hole in the bottom of the boat instead.

Nothing happened. The terns still hovered overhead. For what seemed like an eternity, the sharks remained motionless. Should the motor be started or would it be best to row away? No, I decided, the best thing to do was to remain motionless. Then the sharks decided to move, as if by some common signal or understanding amongst themselves. One shark, almost as if he were the designated leader, made towards the *Kilcullen*; I shuddered as he lazily swam past close by, as if to have a look. Each shark in turn followed, as if also to have a look. Then they all disappeared into the swell on the horizon.

While still shaken with fright, the relief, once the sharks had disappeared, was enormous. It was only afterwards that I remembered the bags of shark repellent somewhere on board. This would have been a good opportunity to try it out since there were conflicting opinions on how effective it was. Should you have the misfortune to be attacked, they say that there is nothing that will stop a shark. All of its senses, bar the sonar sense as he homes in on the target, are switched off. Happily though, many sharks in the ocean are harmless. Recent dramatic films such as *Jaws* have overstated their danger as attackers and killers. Increasingly as the voyage continued I came more to grips with the life and storms of the sea. Sharks can be as frightened or as curious about you as you are of them. In most cases if you leave them alone they will leave you alone.

While later in mid ocean there would be less evidence of marine life, the *Kilcullen* was still close to the edge of the Grand Banks of Newfoundland, an area which is noted for its wealth of sea creatures. On several occasions I would meet porpoises who would follow the *Kilcullen* in a playful manner. They were not large enough to topple the boat so I felt safe in being part of their games; in fact they were fun and playful company and a welcome change from the monotony. However, like children, they soon lost interest in their games and moved on, and I would miss them. Several basking sharks would also cruise past from time to time; about 25 foot in length, they were easy to distinguish on account of their protruding dorsal fin—happily they never stayed around too long since one accidental swipe from a tail could capsize the *Kilcullen*.

My attempts to fish were hopeless, with the wrong fishing tackle on board; and as I moved further into the deep I was less likely to catch any.

Like land, the sea too has mountains and valleys way down in its dark depths. However the reverse is true about these mountains in the sea in that growth thrives on the mountain tops, or in shallower water, while on land the tops of mountains are barren, with fertile valleys. The sea life on these ocean shelves such as the Grand Banks is staggering.

When the sea was calm, we often encountered plastic bags, streaks of oil and dangerous objects floating. This was sad and sickening to see in such a vast area of water; an unfortunate way to be reminded that one is never far from 'civilization'.

I kept my eyes skinned for the elusive Gulf Stream as though it were a river flowing across the Atlantic plains. The stream in fact flows around the Grand Banks, which divert it east after its haul north from the Gulf of Mexico where it originates. It's like a river flowing between banks of cold water—spreading out and becoming more unpredictable the further it goes. Off Florida, for instance, it is only twenty miles wide and flows sometimes in excess of two knots. After 3,000 miles, with the Atlantic crossing behind it, the Stream spreads out over an area some three or four hundred miles wide as it splits up. One part goes north around Ireland and Scotland while the other part takes off south for Spain. Collectively the Stream's climatic influence on Europe is dramatic and much greater than many realize. Without it, Ireland and Britain—being on latitudes even further north than Newfoundland which is iced-in for much of the year, would indeed be barren places. Besides warming the water and keeping the ice away, it forms a block to the constant polar weather systems that sweep down from the north. For places as far north as Bantry Bay or the south-west coast of England, the sight of sub-tropical vegetation from seeds washed up is totally unexpected. This is in extreme contrast to areas like Cape Sable, 300 miles further south, where the Labrador current brings massive ice flows, primitive survival conditions and cold thick fog for much of the year.

In some of my more meditative evenings on board the *Kilcullen,* very preoccupied with the Stream, I spent time trying to imagine the effect if some crazy technocrat diverted the flow of the Stream at source. I had visions of building massive dams off the coast of Florida underwater to divert it, massive explosive charges and so forth; in there somewhere there must be a good plot for a science fiction novel.

Next came the diarrhoea. On reflection it is difficult to know what brought it on. Could it have been the constant worry, or the peanuts combined with chocolate and raisins in my diet, or the whole lot combined? During the cold nights, as I huddled under the canvas cover, it was sheer misery peeling off the many layers of clothes for the cheeks of my arse to meet the rough edges of a bucket that was too small anyway. Not that my rear end is largely proportioned, it's just that I made a big mistake in not buying a wide enough bucket, though the depth was adequate. And to stick my rump over the side in the middle of the night, apart from the cold, was awkward and potentially dangerous.

It took a full twenty-four hours before I remembered the first-aid kit fitted out by Tom Bryan of Connemara and Washington DC and found some special tablets which did the trick. The tablets cured the diarrhoea in under half an hour. Tom had written instructions for all sorts of ailments I never thought possible; happily, though, the salt and sea air kill most internal bugs stone dead in their nasty tracks. Nevertheless, it was consoling to have the kit and nice to know that I had the gear to stitch up a cut or fix a broken leg should the need arise. It would be hard, I thought, to do a worse job stitching myself than a young inexperienced doctor did to me once after I had wrapped a motor car around an unfriendly telegraph pole.

It was around this time, as my mind began to wander, that the *Kilcullen* branch of the Atlantic Residents' Association was formed, otherwise the ARA. It is amazing how the human mind can entertain itself.

'I think that we should form a very liberal society and make all our neighbours welcome to join,' the Social Affairs Minister proposed.

'I disagree, it should be very selective,' the Justice Minister retorted, and so the arguments raged.

Eventually it was decided that, in order to protect the interests of the human inhabitants of the area (me) only humans could join. However in a compromise, sharks, whales and porpoises were granted associate membership with limited voting powers. In fact, seeing that it looked likely that I was set to spend a long period of time on this Atlantic, I determined actually to attend the inaugural meeting in person and actually agreed to join the committee and in due course was elected Finance Minister. In fact, as it transpired, this was a cushy number, in that the unit of currency was fresh air—and that we had in abundance—making us all very rich indeed.

And so it went on for nearly two months. Whenever anything went wrong a meeting was called and the problem was carefully studied before I rushed in to doing anything. Subconsciously, I suppose, this was the single-handed sailor's way of forcing a 'stop and think' approach when any quick or possibly risky decisions had to be made. On the entertainment side, it is amazing how the human mind, when left to its own devices, will look after itself.

One evening at one of the regular meetings, before discussing the most sensible approach to opening a can of beans, the Minister for Health advised all full members to take regular exercise to keep physically in shape. This I started to do regularly when conditions permitted. Another good suggestion he came up with was isometrics when sea conditions were bad, making physical exercise dangerous and difficult. This is a form of stationary exercise where you tense different muscles for a short period of time. They worked well and were also good for the mind.

Before I knew it the water had changed colour, the air was perceptibly warmer and every so often the *Kilcullen* encountered small chunks of light brown tropical seaweed, thousands of miles from its original habitat. I needed no thermometer to tell me that we had reached the Stream. It seemed prudent to refrain from celebrating until the moment when the rough centre of the Stream would be reached and with it the time to alter course a few degrees eastwards, straight for home.

The evening sunset was magical. The sun sank like a great big ball of fire plunging into the sea, the glow and colours spread across the horizon—streaked either side of the fireball—as if marking the end to life as we know it and the start of eternity. Of course the thing sets every night and has been doing so since the beginning of time, and I sincerely hope it continues, but each individual setting is unique and special and retains its own magic.

The morning of August 9th produced another excellent day. I was in high spirits: it would now be simply plain sailing as I rode the warm Gulf Stream all the way to Galway. Our noon latitude put the *Kilcullen* at 40° 50′ N. which is further south than Boston. We glided along beautifully in the warm sun on a north-easterly course with the port lee board half-way down, balanced by the rudder. It was celebration time and the bottle of Mateus Rosé was opened, making me quietly merry as I pigged-out the remaining sweets, chocolate biscuits and a large can of pears.

The following morning was a different story and it was cold again. It blew like stink and the seas started to build. The wind had shifted and the sky was darkened by thick, black and turbulent clouds rolling in. There was something nasty brewing and after a hasty council meeting all sails were dropped, everything was lashed down and I started to take on water ballast. The wind change also brought a confused sea. The *Kilcullen* rolled like a drunken sailor.

I have always been proud of having a good stomach for the sea, and so far on the voyage, apart from a little queasiness, seasickness had not struck. Now it did. It's something I'm told that happens to the best of sailors; something you've just got to learn to handle and get over in spite of the misery it brings.

Being sick on a fully crewed yacht is bad enough but alone at sea it is a great deal more of a worry. There is nobody there to take your place and it is all too easy to get depressed and lose all desire to survive. The storm raged on. To stay alert was a desperate struggle. Every moment was a fight. I forced myself to eat, but that was useless and a waste: no sooner was the hot stew down than it came up again.

But it's amazing how an emergency can galvanize your mind, and how your mind, to cope with it, can overcome the weaknesses of the body. Emergency came with a great mother of a wave that broke, smashing down over the stern and leaving the spare rudder—the only serviceable rudder—askew. The pintle had broken and there was no spare pintle, but with a vice-grip I managed to bend a stainless-steel plate and then bolt it through the rudder so that it held the pintle in place. For a time it held.

By midnight, after raging all day, the worst of the storm was over, with the wind again going around to the south, and I reset the sails and steered again on a north-easterly course.

All through the next day progress continued good—too good, for the water was growing noticeably colder and apparently I was losing the Gulf Stream. Strange, I thought; the course should be keeping me in the Stream. It must just be the Stream meandering, what else could it be?

Luckily there was a clear sun after the storm and I got a few good sights, and from these an accurate fix. It was a shock to discover that somehow I was much further north than I should have been. I was maddened and frustrated. 'What's wrong with my navigation?' I kept asking myself, and I started roaring and screaming. 'You bloody fool! You're lost!' There seemed no possible explanation; the maze of figures and tables were confusing, and there was nobody to ask or to check my calculations. It was only after endless repetition of the arithmetic that I finally discovered the fundamental error—an elementary one that every sailor learns early to avoid. In many parts of the world the magnetic north that a compass shows is not the true north. The difference—the magnetic variation as it's called—is well known and well charted. In the longitude where I was the magnetic north was 24° west of true north—and instead of adding these degrees in my calculations I had somehow managed to subtract them, not just ignoring the error, but doubling it. For several days, the *Kilcullen* had been sailing almost 50° off course!

Now the hard-won miles of southing against the winds had been lost. It would be another long struggle to get back into the Gulf Stream, with the colder water sapping more of my strength and the turbulent, squally verge of the Stream to sail through again.

Immediately I set the lee-board right down to give it the maximum grip on the water and allow me to sail as close to the wind as possible. Now with progress so agonisingly slow it was just not healthy to go on logging my progress every few hours as I had grown accustomed to do, calculating speed and distance run and how long and how far there was to go. Close-hauled and regaining my southing inch by inch, it was better not to know how slow was my progress but to occupy my mind with the Atlantic Residents' Association and all its sub-committees and administrative problems.

Of all the books I had with me, James Joyce's *Ulysses* was the most complex, confusing, boring and stupid. What people saw in it defied my simple mind.

However, having heard so much about the book, I was determined to finish it. Literature is for the literate, I suppose, or for those who consider themselves literate, and as I ploughed on through the turgid, intricate stuff I was forced to the conclusion that I must resign myself to being among the great unlettered.

Once, resting my eyes from Mr Joyce and feasting them on the marching Atlantic ridges, I saw the humped back and fin of a big fish in the distance. Dolphin or shark, I thought, but as it appeared and reappeared nearer and nearer, I changed my mind: it could only be a whale. Every so often jets of water could be seen from the enormous mammal between the waves, and it came so close I could see the animal itself just below the surface, like a small barren island regurgitated by the sea. Once the wind caught the jet and sprayed it close by me. The smell reminded me of a fish factory with its warm, rank fishy tang; and indeed I suppose the whale was nothing more or less than a factory, processing its huge daily intake of seafood.

I was trembling with fear and at the same time excited at seeing the great mammal, so majestic and yet so graceful and so unreal. Then suddenly it turned its head to point straight at the *Kilcullen,* and it moved towards me at a slow, menacing pace. I froze tense, grasping the nearest rope and waited. Then, when it was only feet away from me, the giant dived. Not the lissome, frolicking dive of a porpoise or a dolphin, but the steady, powerful, sinking submersion of a submarine.

I could feel the effect of suction in the water as the whale disappeared beneath me and a slight stir as it passed under the boat. Helpless, I waited, wondering where he would surface and what would happen if he chose my particular spot in the ocean to do so in. Nothing happened, and I never saw that whale again; he must have surfaced half a mile away or more, out of my sight, to scare the living daylights out of some other unsuspecting creature.

Not many people have seen a whale at close quarters from a small boat. Like anything unknown and unexpected it can be very frightening, but then again I have read that they are harmless creatures if you leave them alone; those that have used their giant strength to sink whale-boats with a stroke of their tails must have been attacked first. From the little that so-called *homo sapiens* knows about these mammals, they seem to be extraordinarily intelligent, and to move and communicate in a world of acoustics known only to them. Like all mammals they breathe air, and the spout that first reveals their presence is, of course, their exhalation through blowholes (usually two) neatly provided in their back. Oddly enough many more whale spouts can be seen on windy days than when it is calm, the reason being that in rougher weather there are more waves washing over the creatures' backs as they lie breaking the surface.

Peacefulness seems the word best to characterize a school of whales: observations seem to show that they are easy-going and not in the least aggressive. Even when they do compete, as for mating purposes, they do it gently. The bond between the mother whale and calf is one of the subtlest and most moving ties on earth, and it is sad to think that this bond is one that the whaling industry uses for its purposes. A calf swims slower than its mother and can be more easily approached by the harpooners. The loving bond outweighs intelligence, for the mother will never abandon her young, and its agony is used to draw the frantic mother within harpoon range.

Relentless hunting with such vicious tactics has all but eradicated many types of whale, and now a growing number of nations is slowly waking up and beginning to protect them. But will it be too late?

A youth was shot dead on the eve of the Queen's visit to Northern Ireland. Yesterday, after an enormous security exercise, she and the Duke of Edinburgh completed the first day of their historic 36-hour tour without incident. So I heard on the transistor radio, for once picking up the BBC World Service clearly. It must have been some freak spot on the ocean, for generally the *Kilcullen,* so close to the surface that I could not pick up a good signal, was quite cut off from the rest of the world.

The voice from the little box told me that the Queen had had her first ride in a helicopter, and now she was meeting the Nobel Prize-winning leaders of the Peace People for tea on the royal yacht *Britannia.* Perhaps, I thought, she might fly out in her little chopper and join the lonely skipper of the *Kilcullen* for a spot of tea as well? No sooner was it framed than the formal invitation was approved by the social committee of the Atlantic Residents' Association, who instructed the Hon. Secretary and scribe to draft it in properly regal terms and deposit it in the empty champagne bottle when I had celebrated half-way point.

The night was cold with a sort of haze, not quite a fog. Just after dark there was a far-off thumping noise, like the sound from a low-rev., but massive water pump. It was a ship, and I could see its outline distinctly in the haze. For a while I feared it was coming straight for me but bit by bit the outline changed shape and I realized she was steering a parallel course, slowly overtaking me. The glazed lights of the after cabins as she moved ahead of me stirred up thoughts of company, good food and a spring bed. I was like a little tinker boy staring through a window at a warm happy family party during Christmastime.

Why was the ship moving so slowly? The deep thumping sound as she took half an hour to overtake me was somehow disconcerting. It wasn't until the following morning that the reason for her cautious speed was explained: far off in the distance I saw the dazzling gleam of an iceberg.

When I was planning the voyage the thought of encountering icebergs was exciting. These massive floating islands have been known to drift far south before melting, and certainly the *Kilcullen* was now well inside the ice region. The water for miles around a berg is cold, and I certainly felt it, but I had no fear of encountering one: I was in the only sort of boat in the world that would just bounce off.

My first plan had been to head for the first berg I saw and plant a bottle of Canadian Club whiskey on it, with a bottle of Guinness for company. When it came to the point, however, I chickened out, thinking of the dangerous swell that would surround the berg and the sharp slivers of ice I just might meet. Later I regretted not having taken the chance to be one of the few to get to know an iceberg at close quarters from a dinghy, and once I was back in the warm Gulf Stream waters I didn't see another berg for the rest of the voyage.

The wind was now from the north-west, ideal for working south and back into the main body of the Stream. There were some vicious thunderstorms, complete with the strong squalls and downpours of rain that belong to them, but these squalls were not so hard to handle as a gale of the same force, for there was seldom time for the seas to build up. When sunshine came in bursts of an hour or two, it was a matter of making as much use of it as possible for navigating and drying out. Pleasure or misery depended on each cloud formation, and these squalls galloped up and overtook me at an alarming rate.

I could not have picked a worse place to cross the turbulent forty miles or so where the two great currents meet: the warm east-going waters from the Gulf, and the cold south-westerly Labrador current. I was at about latitude 43° N., 50° W. which is at the very tip of the Grand Banks and the North American ocean shelf, where the two great currents, following the contours of the sea-bed, converge in chaos and confusion.

Such a chop and unsettled water seemed strange four hundred

miles from land, for they are the sort of sea conditions more commonly met offshore, perhaps where an outflowing river meets an inflowing tide in relatively shallow water. I suppose the turbulence would hardly be noticeable in larger boats, but for a small dinghy this part of the Atlantic is to be avoided at all costs. I was learning the hard way, but luckily the wind was moderate; I would hate to be in that area in a storm.

Back in the Gulf Stream, things warmed up. The never-ending swell was big, but the crests were farther apart, marching effort- lessly on across the ocean with nothing to disturb their enormous rhythm.

By August 16th the wind had dropped off completely, and I was becalmed in the warm sea and sun, drifting imperceptibly east at exactly 0.8 knots with the stream. It was a much needed chance to recuperate, relax and dry out as the Newfoundland radio stations bit by bit became faint and disappeared altogether from the reach of my little transistor.

As I strained to hear the last news bulletins, the self-styled 'Son of Sam', who had terrorized New York, was arrested by police; caught, after killing six and wounding seven young people, in one of the biggest manhunts the city had seen. The loner Son of Sam lived in Yonkers, one of New York's many massive sprawling suburbs. Was he the product of the isolation and loneli- ness of big-city living? Of television violence? Or of the fiercely competitive, cut-throat environment, of the unnatural herding together of men? The media had a peculiar way of glamorizing him, capitalizing on people's fears to turn him into a celebrity.

He was alone with seven million New Yorkers of all nation- alities and types, their interest in him ephemeral. He was soon to be crushed and forgotten among them. I was alone with just seven million more ridges of salt swell; with a never-ending horizon and equally uncaring nature. Which of us was better off, I wondered?

A medium-sized container ship flying the Dutch flag came in sight, but the rust and streaks of old paint on her sides made it impossible to read her name. She approached and slowly came right up to me, within shouting distance, and I yelled the *Kilcul- len*'s name and destination and asked to be reported. This was never done, maybe because they couldn't understand my English. Once the Captain saw that everything seemed in order he quickly went on his way. Unlike the crew of an American ship I was to meet later, the Dutch crew seemed oddly uninterested in the curious sight of a mad Irishman in a rubber boat in the middle of the Atlantic. So what? their expression seemed to say.

By contrast the Americans were all excited and spurred into action, everyone tearing around on deck, waving or finding lifebelts or taking pictures.

My cold, unsatisfactorily encounter with the Dutch ship seemed formally to mark my entry into the real isolation of mid Atlantic. In a way it was a peaceful period: the calm before the storm.

8

Point of no return

STILL MOVING further out into the Atlantic isolation the *Kilcullen* had gone beyond the point of no return. Each day crawled past and crawled into weeks; but for the fact that it was necessary to navigate, getting sunsights when possible from the plastic sextant, I would have lost all track of time.

The constant movement, wear and tear each day caused concern that all the tubes would eventually start leaking. Likewise since it was a glorified liferaft, there was no additional liferaft, or last resort, on board that a normal sailing boat would have crossing an ocean.

In the interest of progress I was starting to become more adventurous and, in some respects careless. Again, just when it had seemed that the weather had settled, the wind and waves started to build from the south-west. In vain I tried to apply Ballot's Law which is a rule-of-thumb method of determining the path of the centre of a depression. In theory, once the path of the centre is determined, you can navigate your boat to the least dangerous part of the depression. Sadly though, since the *Kilcullen* was so slow, we had to take the full fury of whatever God served up regardless.

A neighbour in Galway, Commander Bill King, on his first circumnavigation attempt on *Galway Blazer,* spoke with horror of his voyage through the eye of a hurricane in the South Atlantic.

'There were great mountains of seas and then there was calm, it was uncanny. The wind just disappeared.'

Bill went on to describe his horror when the wind filled in again, this time with increased fury, from another direction. 'There were walls of water, the waves were going straight up in the air, there was such turbulence with the wind and waves going in opposite directions.' Not surprisingly, this was more than the 35ft *Galway Blazer* could handle. She was rolled and dismasted. Fortunately Bill came out OK, having been trapped inside, since the boat was virtually built like a submarine anyway. Happily the great Commander made it to safety and lived to tell the tale in addition to being the sole surviving submarine commander from the Second World War who seemed to have kept his sanity.

Would I? For meanwhile, it seemed, I was going crazy. The stern wind was increasing to near gale force and still the sails remained up. The *Kilcullen* surfed along furiously at an average speed of five knots. At this rate we would be home in two weeks. There was a call for an ARA meeting but it was ignored. Spray was flying and the waves were breaking around and still I kept going. I simply cared no longer; foolishly I was pushing everything to the limit. Perhaps it was a subconscious decision to keep moving, to keep occupied with sailing the boat. The alternative, as in previous gales, was bleak. With the sails down, I would be alone and unoccupied, trapped with my thoughts and fears as I was tossed around in the waves, huddled up under the canvas cover.

Then the heavens erupted. Buckets of rain, enough to convert the Sahara Desert into a green pasture full of fat cows, poured down. From above and below, virtually everything was soaked wet. And while the thundering rain pacified the howling winds temporarily, it returned with increased fury after.

But still I persisted with my madness with sails up, carefully getting the stern under each wave and surfing down it. Then, like falling off a three-story building, the *Kilcullen* literally fell off a wave. It was almost a miracle dispatched personally by God from heaven that she didn't flip. Instead the wooden floorboards were ruptured on impact. This put my heart sideways in my mouth and brought an abrupt halt to the madness as I climbed up along the tube to remove the sails. Another wave swept me overboard but I was well secured with the strong safety harness line bolted to the wooden transom; within seconds I had bounced back on board again.

Then, as we slid sideways off another wave, the rudder broke and the pintle was smashed. Now the *Kilcullen* was totally out of control, at the mercy of the elements. A wave broke over

1. In Chesapeake Bay *Kilcullen (I)* undergoes sailing trials.

2. Marblehead, Mass. *Kilcullen (I)* complete with all gear and equipment, ready for departure. All she needs is inflation.

3. Steering problems in *Kilcullen (I)*. The tiller is lashed by splints and fishing line. The spare leeboard is lashed to the outboard motor to make an excellent emergency rudder.

4. A shark scrapes under the bottom of the boat, scaring the living daylights out of me.

5. My camera survived the capsize. Rare shot of the stormy Atlantic as taken from capsized inflatable.

6. Inverted *Kilcullen (I)* and liferaft ready to be hauled aboard rescue ship, the Royal Fleet Auxiliary Ship *Stromness*.

7. At Plymouth, *Kilcullen (I)* is packed up on board H.M.S. *Ambuscade* for transit home via British Rail and a sail across the Irish Sea.

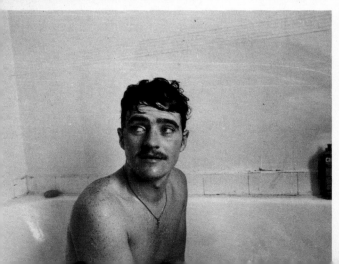

8. Back home, my first press conference was given, in view of pressing evening deadlines, while I was having a bath.

the transom, filling the boat with water, then she lay broadside on, awash. Still the seas got bigger, the wind increased and from time to time would scatter breaking wave tops in clouds of spray for many yards at a time. Cold, wet and miserable, with a totally helpless feeling, I huddled up under the canvas cover in an effort to stay warm and conserve heat. Even the Atlantic Residents' Association remained silent; this was not a time to be amusing, the *Kilcullen*'s situation and that of her skipper was very serious indeed.

I'd like to be tough and brave and say that I was not frightened but the reality is that I was terrified. There was no way of telling how strong the wind was but I was not alone. In the lee of the *Kilcullen* about half a dozen seabirds took advantage of the little shelter there was. With each wave they bobbed up and down, oblivious to the fears and dangers running through my mind. Though side by side, it was me who was the stranger, outside of his natural habitat, intruding on their vast world of water. God, bless him, was there too; into his hands my life and the safety of the boat was placed.

That day stretched on forever. The night lasted longer again. The winds howled and I hunched in a ball, knees into my chest, under the cover. Not being able to see the waves was terrifying, though the sound of each described them adequately. I prayed. I also thought a lot of the simple things in life that we take for granted, such as sitting on a comfortable steady chair. I escaped into visions of sitting in an enormous armchair in front of a turf fire with a pipe full of fine tobacco and my legs up.

In terms of survival, the breaking of the rudder was a blessing in disguise in that it left the *Kilcullen* totally out of control, simply sliding off the waves and surviving the storm like a cork. However, what would happen after the seas and wind eased? How could the *Kilcullen* be steered? There was no well stocked workshop available or the bits to complete this repair 700 miles out into the ocean.

At dawn the following day, with great difficulty, I made a cup of coffee. Fortunately one box of supplies in the centre of the boat had remained reasonably dry. However just as I was about to sink a hot drink after the struggle to make it, a section of the lashed sail worked loose, and that had to be secured quickly. In the process the drink spilled and I took some spray, losing all of the built-up heat. The salt water was rough and cutting.

I began to hate the sea. Eventually, after the storm had passed, the process of rehabilitation and restoration of confidence began. The rudder problem was solved by making the outboard motor into a rudder. I lashed the spare leeboard to the side of the motor shaft. The dislocated floorboards were also a major problem. In addition to the discomfort element, by being out of place, they would cause uneven wear on the tubes. To fix them back would involve deflating the boat completely. The A.R.A., after some debate, advised against. However by partial deflation it was possible to get them back some of the way. Likewise, though it was a nuisance having to top up the tubes every few hours, the exercise was good, and the leaks—provided they were not going to get any worse—were no cause for concern.

The following day a ship appeared right on the *Kilcullen*'s course. She was an American container ship. She stopped. The swell was still large and, using the oars, I went as close as I dared. By this time it seemed that many of the crew lined the decks in their lifejackets and were expecting to rescue me. Twelve hours earlier, perhaps, but not now; though the temptation was there.

'Please send word home and say that we're in good shape,' I roared. This the Captain of the M.V. *Lightning* out of New York kindly did. That position report was 43° 20′ N., 46° 08′ W. Later I learned that that position report brought much relief to many people on both side of the Atlantic who were concerned about the safety of the *Kilcullen* following the storm. It would be a long time before they would hear again and later, I would very much regret not asking the Captain for some food to top up the dwindling food supplies.

The cassette tape recorder could stand the hardship no more and gave up the ghost, so with little ceremony it got dumped overboard. Happily though, the transistor radio remained in working order and, though out of reach of most stations, it was possible to get the BBC World Service, the Voice of America and Radio Moscow from time to time. This was good company . . .

'Two hundred thousand tourists in Spain are stranded in hotel workers' strike ...The National Front organizes massive demonstration in Birmingham . . .' All this served to take my mind off the grim reality on board the *Kilcullen*.

The dislocated floorboards made sleeping uncomfortable, the air-bed having long since burst; not by any extra nocturnal activity, I might add, rather owing to a sharp edge. Every day there seemed to be something breaking. I stitched the mizzen sail in areas which were likely to tear from the flogging, then there was the canvas cover in which the D rings holding it up to form a tent arch were working loose . . . there was no end to it. The most recent being a leeboard which snapped in half due to the load—leaving a rough edge. Since it happened in darkness I decided to leave it until morning; this was a mistake and, as a result of the chafing which followed, it almost sank the inflatable.

Other damage was not so serious but it all added up. The end of the sprit for the mizzen sail fell out and I made good the loss by shoving in a toothbrush. Time and time again I was amazed by the great number of repairs I made which, in normal circumstances, would not be thought of. I had few tools, and many of those rusted, but when put to the test, many improvisations worked. They had to. It's amazing what we can do as individuals, whatever situation we may be involved with, when we have to. This, I suppose, was the element of challenge which was pleasing.

Again the weather settled. Was the worst over? Certainly there was not much left to frighten the *Kilcullen*'s skipper. As long as the boat and her skipper could take the punishment it was simply a matter of time. Not much seemed to matter any more. The hours and days simply dragged on to the point where mentally I was slipping into another world. My mind would wander and would climb out of my body and look at me. It was weird and dangerous.

A great concern with seafarers has always been to keep the matches dry. I thought I was smart in getting over this problem by taking a bunch of disposable cigarette lighters, only to discover that the salt air swiftly corroded all of the flints. Not being able to heat a can of meat or make a hot drink any more was more damaging psychologically than any other way, since, in the end, the food does the same thing, hot or cold. Happily from the remaining lighters and bits of flints I managed to get just one working which was then stored in an inside pocket close to my chest and miraculously kept the *Kilcullen* in naked flame for the remainder of the voyage.

Little things started to get on my nerves such as the vacuum flask which had slipped under the floorboards when we fell off the waves, and now, adrift between the rubber bottom and the board, it kept knocking.

'You must keep going, you must not give up, fight, fight fight . . .' I kept telling myself. At times I would shout out loud, rant and rave around the limited floor space but who cares? Nobody hears anyway and at least it keeps the voice in shape!

The next carrot on the route was the imaginary half-way mark and the bottle of champagne which was waiting to be demolished. In actual fact, the half-way mark inserted on the chart was more than half-way at 35° longitude; my grabbing mentality always likes to have something in reserve.

Indeed the pilot chart of the North Atlantic is a fascinating document, packed with information for the navigator and voyager. On it is marked the average wind directions for each area over the past thirty years, the average temperatures, ocean currents, iceberg zones, storm tracks, shipping lanes, magnetic variation and so forth. For hours on end I would stare at it, pondering over everything. Navigation and the noon fix, almost like that of a drug addict, was a high point each day. It was also around that time that I discovered the shit, grass, marijuana—or whatever you like to call it—packed in with my food in a plastic bag, evidently stuffed in there by some of the drug people I met in Halifax. Would it be dangerous to smoke it and get high?

Happily the weather was warming up considerably, we were now into our fourth week since departing Halifax and, all going well, another three weeks should bring the *Kilcullen* close to a landfall. But the wind dropped away.

'Not to worry,' I told the giant albatross who hovered overhead, watching like a hawk for any discarded scraps.

'Now is a good time for a wash and to get everything dried out completely,' or some such words I would constantly yatter on, talking to myself and the skipper of the now, unsinkable *Kilcullen*. Of course with the salt air and salt in virtually everything, absorbing the humidity, it was impossible to get the dampness out. Indeed this dampness, constantly close to the skin, was starting to cause considerable discomfort and salt sores.

Therefore, standing in the nude was heaven on earth. So free in the teaming warm sun at the seaside, my very own little world in the sea. 'So what if there is no wind, let's be free and enjoy the sun and warmth while it's there,' the gathering of the Atlantic Residents' Association was informed at the daily navigation meeting.

The sky was beautiful and clear. Yet again the colossal size and force of this ocean, and all oceans covering two thirds of the earth, is driven home. Its moods; the colossal force of a single wave built up over thousands of interrupted miles by the almighty power of the invisible wind. Then complete tranquillity. Nothing to disturb it for hundreds of miles in either direction on a calm day. Its great beauty and treachery is conflicting. Of course we all know that the oceans are vast, like the deserts of the world, but it's only when you're right out there—in my case on its own level, separated just by an air tube—that the sheer size comes home to roost in the subconscious. It gives an awesome, overpowering, exciting feeling all at once.

It is Tristan Jones who sums up many feelings seafarers have for the sea when he says: 'I can never love the sea, any more than I can love the air, or the stars in space. I can only love what I think about them. How can I love something that isolates me from all things that I truly love? Good company, intricate conversation, live music, the welter of art, and people, people, people—and all their ways of wonder—and children, and the dream of the future. What does the sea know of them?'

'I know full well what it is that I love—that I love about the sea. It is the illusion of mastery, the pride of skill; and the seafaring life itself. But the sea herself—never.'

On this day the sea was seductive. Come in, she was saying; so I decided for a swim, having first scanned the horizon for sharks. It was also a good opportunity to wash and scrub the growth off *Kilcullen*'s bottom.

It was blissful. Stark naked in the flat, clear sea, the freedom was exhilarating as I trod water from a short distance watching my inflatable home bob up and down in the gentle swell. For safety I had a long rope hanging loose floating in the water to grab hold of, should a puff of wind suddenly blow the *Kilcullen* out of reach. Being also concerned by the extra chafing caused by the broken leeboard, it seemed an appropriate time to check for wear on the side of the tube, which was just as well. I was shocked to discover a significant area of the fabric almost worn right through to the nylon weave, below the waterline. Unchecked, within days, it would be worn completely through. But how was it to be patched underwater? Mending it above the surface would be hard enough, but this was an impossible situation.

The happy humour of the morning took a nose dive as I climbed back on board and cursed my luck.

'Get yourself out of this one, you silly fool.'

'Shut up, you negative jerk,' my subconscious replied before a plan of action emerged. It was critical to get it done before the wind filled in, which was inevitable with some cloud formations developing on the western horizon.

Firstly all the gear and stores were transferred to one side but this was not quite enough to get the worn part clear of the water. Then empty water and fuel containers were submerged under the tube to lift it further out of the sea which did the trick. Next I donned a lifejacket and, treading water in the cold ocean for over half an hour, I eventually secured a patch. I was much relieved.

In patching an inflatable boat there is much more to it than meets the eye, in particular surface preparation plays an important part. In this respect the six weeks spent training in the Zodiac service shop proved invaluable. Happily the evening remained calm and I kept the patch dry for as long as possible.

That evening, instead of the wind filling in from the west as expected it blew from the east, blowing the *Kilcullen* backwards since it was not possible to sail into the wind. Instead, I streamed a sea-anchor, which is a small parachute underwater to stop drift. And, while not stopping, it slowed down our backwards progress significantly. In fact I had several of these sea-anchors, the theory being that they hold the bow into the wind which prevents you turning beam on and capsizing in a storm. Later, much to my cost, I was to learn that this was most definitely not the way to ride out a gale, easterly or not, on this inflatable and probably on other boats her size.

Fortunately there was no storm blowing and the easterly swung around within twelve hours to a south westerly direction, sails were set once more, and the *Kilcullen* was on her way.

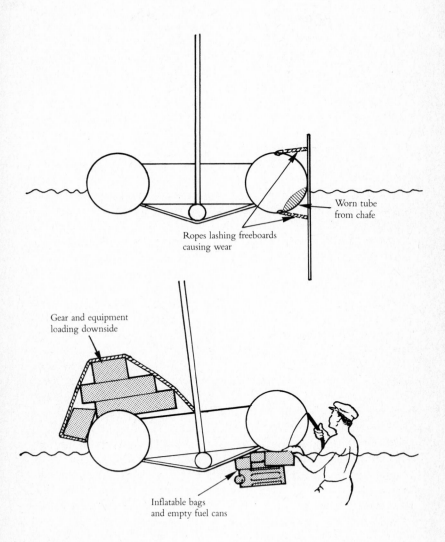

Worn tube
from chafe

Ropes lashing freeboards
causing wear

Gear and equipment
loading downside

Inflatable bags
and empty fuel cans

Repairs at Sea

And if taking pleasure is regarded as sin, I'm guilty in so far as I had an affair with my sextant; the fact that she was only of plastic did not concern me. Navigation gave great satisfaction, particularily with plenty of sun about the place. Each day I felt more accomplished at it using the sextant. Height from sea level helps and being so low was a problem; likewise the constant movement of the dinghy made it difficult to remain steady long enough for a good fix. But fix I did, measuring some accurate angles between the sun and horizon in the process. Here the safety harness would come in useful in giving freedom to stand on one of the tubes. With split second timing, on top of a wave, it was necessary to make the lower rim of the sun coincide with the line of the horizon by adjusting the arm of the sextant so that they appeared in the eye-piece in exaxt juxtaposition. While doing all that, it was necessary to take the time, accurate to the second, each of these seconds being necessary for accuracy in working out lines of position.

Then with a good fix, the details of working through the damp and sometimes waterlogged tables absorbed many hours of the day. This was only necessary for longitude while latitude, taken from the noon sight when the sun was at its highest, was a much simpler affair.

Then the *Kilcullen's* long awaited imaginary half-way mark came and went. It was celebrated at an arbitrary time and the day I chose, I think, was 26 August. In advance I had written a long note to seal in the bottle of champagne after demolishing it. In reality I was engaging in a form of subconscious self-deception, playing off the split-personality on board. The thinking behind it was that really the *Kilcullen* was beyond the half-way mark, a fact which I would not let on to myself. In this way there was always something extra in reserve and all on board would be pleasantly surprised when the voyage and landfall would be completed sooner.

Of course, on popping the champagne cork, it exploded into the air and, much to the frustration of all on board, there was nothing left to seal the note in. Then, well secured by the harness, I allowed myself to get merry and ran a singsong before dropping off to sleep. On awakening with a jolt, for no apparent reason, in the middle of the night lying under the stars, my head hurt. Happily and regardless of the hangover, the *Kilcullen* cruised along, left to her own devices. I dreamed a lot and recall a great feeling of satisfaction at this point and on having come so far, against the odds. But I was alone, there was nobody there to share the celebration with, making it all seem worthless.

Is this selfish? Selfish in not sharing this beautiful tranquil world? Selfish in not thinking of others who were constantly worried about my welfare back in civilization? Frankly, I had never considered myself worth worrying about. To this day I never cease to be amazed, and flattered, that so many people were constantly concerned and praying. Rosaries, prayers and stations of the cross were done on my behalf by family, neighbours, friends and even strangers. However, not wishing to sound malicious, facetious or ungrateful, I can't help feeling that many people must have had little else to be worried about. An unusual voyage such as the *Kilcullen*'s, with its genuine adventure element, gave something new to identify with in comparison to the normal things that people are concerned about.

Did praying help? Did you ever pray? people ask. Quite honestly I don't know. Completely atheistic men have gone alone for longer periods of time and faced greater dangers. They survived to tell their tales, giving little credit to God in the process. Other survivors are convinced that but for God and prayer they would never have made it. More write off God as a psychological invention and a created necessity to fill a gap, to fill the need for something supernatural, something beyond the ordinary. Perhaps.

The voyage of the *Kilcullen* convinced me, though, that there is a God. No intelligent thinking human being can, in all honesty, disbelieve the existence of God. Who has the correct interpretation of this God is something mankind has been fighting about since the beginning of time, and in the fable since Adam grabbed that apple in the garden of Eden. I like to think that everybody's God is the correct one.

Another week passed. It was now September. People often ask, was I ever bored. The answer is rarely, if ever. This adventure formed a separate compartment in my brain and, although each day seemed to have no limit, time had lost all relative importance. All points of reference on which to base the passage of the day, such as meetings or the day's normal timetable, were gone.

Another calm period arrived when the ocean went flat. For

miles in every direction the horizon was clear to the point where sky blends with sea. Secured by the fact that I had not seen any sharks or porpoises for a time, a wash and some dives to scrape the growth off the *Kilcullen*'s bottom was in order. This was made all the more necessary since the special anti-fouling had worn away and the barnacles were thriving, slowing us down in the process.

Scraping the bottom was hard work; it was also cold to be in the water for more than five minutes. Every so often it was necessary to climb back on board to rest, gather thoughts, courage and energy. Holding my breath, treading water and working right under the boat, trapped with nothing but water below for miles, was an eerie feeling. At last, though, the bottom was clean again, bringing with it the satisfaction of a job well done.

There was hardly a breath of wind. The evening sun was warm and the work completed had created a greater confidence in the water with less fears so, after a nice long rest, a leisurely swim was in order. Whether it was the effect of the hard work or the final bottle of Canadian beer, I'll never know, but for that swim I broke the golden rule of keeping a safety line. It was so free, swimming naked in the cool sea, with the bright evening sun heading into the ocean yet again to set on another day. Treading water, my eyes almost level with the sea surface, made the *Kilcullen* look so different. With hardly a bother in the world, she bobbed gently up and down in the swell. A tiny speck on the ocean, a self-contained world. I felt happy and relaxed, becoming part fish, part creature—losing all touch and contact with mankind. Swimming around, perhaps fancying myself as a fish, the fish became more daring and swam further away in a circle. It was exhilarating. Without realizing it, I had drifted further and further away from the inflatable.

A cloud formation arrived and with it a puff of wind started to blow the *Kilcullen* away. Suddenly I realized what was happening and started to swim back to the boat as fast as possible. But she drifted faster as I started to swim faster. Still there was little sign of the gap narrowing. Now, I was swimming for my life, a dramatic change from my tranquil world moments before when I felt like the almighty King.

I swam like a man possessed. Quick enough perhaps for an

Olympic medal. Finally the *Kilcullen* slowed down for me just enough. I clasped the side with a dead man's grip. Minutes later, I gathered enough strength to climb on board and virtually collapse.

For a long time I simply lay there, shaken and cold. The other part of me pranced furiously around the *Kilcullen* shouting, 'You stupid, bloody fool; you should know better at this stage!'

With such a limited number of places to sit and sitting down for so long, a salt sore had developed on my rear end. Now it was starting to hurt. So far, during the voyage, great care had been taken to vary my sitting positions, not only to stop sores developing but also to stop wear on parts of the tubes that I might sit on constantly.

Recovered, dressed, but not altogether with it after the swimming shock, I was searching for various salt sore ointments when I discovered again the few ounces of marijuana weed. Good Columbian stuff, I was told; now I wanted to escape and lit up.

It was indeed an escape into another world. Some joints were rolled and, to use the American expression, I got a big buzz on. The sun that evening was special indeed, hovering like a mighty red ball over the western horizon, its spectrum of colours spread across as far as the eye could see on either side. With the harness around my chest, the *Kilcullen*'s skipper, temporarily out of commission, was well secured to his craft.

A group of porpoises appeared and circled the *Kilcullen* a few times before making off; their company was welcome and their playing no longer put me on edge. Before moving on, to them, the inflatable was just a passing curiosity.

Being dead did not seem to matter anymore. My mind started to go crazy and disappear off into a tropical paradise. Way off on the horizon, in the evening darkness, a little light appeared and then dropped away again. A ship, and its floating world of life, had almost come our way but had gone curving around the horizon again.

'If you're a nibbler you'll be in trouble,' some memorable last words a wee lad uttered shortly before departing the quayside in Halifax. And right he was. Food supplies were dwindling fast; all the time I had tended to nibble all day and eat all the biscuits, chocolate, raisins and other snack-type food, leaving now only the cans of meat and other bits and pieces. That evening, probably as a result of the dope, I must have gone through about a week's supply of food, food that was already being rationed out.

And after all that, following a day that was probably best forgotten, it must have been about twelve hours before I awoke again. By this time the wind had filled in from the east, blowing the *Kilcullen* backwards for over two days, which was soul-destroying. The time was spent doing my nut. While I could happily drift along through the days when progress towards home was being made, this situation was unbearable.

9

Dream vs reality

THE BOTTOM LINE is a singleminded stubbornness. You just simply refuse to give up. Besides, there was no alternative. The more people laughed at my Atlantic Challenge, the more determined I became and now, the sheer size of the ocean was leaving a marked impression.

As the days passed, my mind tended to run on, out of control. Often it was impossible to distinguish between reality, dreams or nightmares. I would get lost in a trance and it would take something dramatic to snap me out of it. Chay Blyth calls it mental plonk. At one moment, for instance, I would decide to open a can of meat. Then nothing would happen for about twenty minutes before action took place, after that it might be another fifteen minutes before the stove was lit and so on.

During the day I would constantly doze off for short spells, while at night for hours I would sit watching the phosphorescence flashing through the night, rivalled only by the stars. The phosphorescence made the entire sea come alive, glowing in the dark like a heap of live coals. It was made up of fish larvae and millions of plankton and the big round moon made it glow in the night sea like a bag of sparkling jewels. Like staring at a fire, for hours on end I would stare at the ocean, a little bit stirred up each time as the *Kilcullen* ploughed along.

It was at night time that the sea came alive with many fish seemingly coming to the surface to eat. During the days, with the sun's rays penetrating, they go deeper and, as if lonely like myself, come to the surface to socialize at night. Like any moving object, slow and all as we may be, the *Kilcullen* attracted followers. An odd time I would switch on the waterproof electric torch, whose batteries were fast fading. The beam would attract the little fish who concentrated in its circle of light. On moving the beam, the fish would move with it.

Then suddenly, while still lost in admiration and playing around with the intricate movements of the small fish, a quick thud made me grab the side of the boat. It was truly a large shark, the upper side of its tail being much longer than the lower. The creature had turned over on its back to swim towards the *Kilcullen* and the light. I looked with horror as its teeth flashed in the light of the torch and its white belly in the moonlight. Whether it was trying to take a bite out of the boat, I do not know, but I have always been told that sharks turned on their backs to seize their prey. I was alarmed and swiftly cut out the light and hoped that the thing would go away. Momentarily its tail continued to beat around the boat like the crack of a whip, splashing sea water all over the place. From time to time over the next few minutes the shark's white stomach could be seen gliding through the phosphorescence and the moonlight; but then, presumably bored by my inactivity, it made off.

That experience drove a hard lesson home in that a torch can be dangerous at night. In fact, using one is an old trick practised by fishermen trying to lure sharks and their friends! There's nothing like learning the hard way—that is, if you survive to tell the tale. This particular shark attack was serious but with the inflatable tubes being as difficult to get one's teeth round as a football, I comforted myself that the shark would be put off. Hopefully, in future, such undesirable guests would keep their distance.

At this stage, the *Kilcullen* was relatively far south, and in order to make Ireland I needed to make a more northerly course. This might have been all very well in July or August but now, penetrating deeper into September, it was to prove a mistake. However another reason to get north was to get back into the main shipping lanes where there would be a better chance of stopping a ship for extra food and of getting a position report home.

But getting into the shipping lanes created its own worries, namely the fear of being run down. While impossible to be seen at night and with not enough power to run a navigation light, it was unlikely that the *Kilcullen* would be picked up during the day either, being so low down, even with the radar reflector. I had my own theory in regard to being run down, though fortunately it was never put to the test. That is, if a ship approached on a collision course, the bow wave would shove me clear, being so small. However the big danger would be at the stern, where, if a small craft were positioned wrong, the massive propellers of a ship would suck you in.

Food and drink were a constant preoccupation: with 800 miles to go, at least sixteen days at fifty miles a day, there would simply not be enough food. It was difficult to know whether to exercise to stay in shape or just to stop and conserve energy on less food. I started to have visions of just bones and flesh crawling up a beach someplace on the west coast of Ireland. On departing, it seemed that there was more food on board than could be eaten, but there had been more setbacks than I ever expected. Fishing was out of the question; I had lost all of my fishing lines by this stage.

Alcohol was another danger and, rightly or wrongly, in a moment of strong will, I threw what was left overboard in addition to the dope and valium tablets in the first-aid kit. My mind, left to it own devices as it strayed into and out of a world of make-believe, was dangerous enough without outside influence. In my imagination I started to visit many pubs and have a pint in each. I spent a great deal of time trying to calculate how one could pass from one side to the other side of my home town, Galway, without passing a public house. Not surprisingly, I failed.

It never ceases to amaze how the mind works and how things we think that we have long forgotten, come back. Over that period of prolonged isolation there was little of my past life that I did not think of, ranging from being expelled from school to being knocked out as a child.

No more sugar left, and I was down to water and cans of beans with meat; in desperation I turned to the two small jars of Bovril which had remained unopened. They were given to me by my Zodiac friend Tim Curtis, who thinks the world of the stuff. And while great mountain climbers like Chris Bonnington are paid vast sums to praise the meal in a jar, I am being polite when I say that I hate the stuff. However, when you're hungry, it's simply amazing what you will eat; the greatest mental challenge was to actually ration rather than eating the whole lot of the remaining food there and then while forgetting about tomorrow. Fortunately there was a plentiful supply of vitamin pills which must have helped considerably.

I used to dream of large steaks, gravy and buckets of fresh new potatoes. Fresh fruit, hot sun and a warm tropical climate forever. The reality was that it was getting colder, the days were getting shorter, my stomach had a hollow ring and the skies were starting to look unfriendly indeed.

If you'll forgive the expression, my personal hygiene was also deteriorating and at times I felt like the proverbial pig in shit. For some reason the story of the drunk man at the pig fair in rural Ireland comes into mind. It too was September:

> 'September, the day I well remember
> I walked up the street in drunken pride.
> My knees began to flutter
> And I fell down the gutter
> And, as I lay there in the gutter, thinking thoughts that I dare not utter, a great big fat pig picked me up and lay down by my side. Then I heard a passing lady say:
> 'You can tell the man who boozes
> By the company that he chooses,'
> And with that the pig got up and walked away.

Like the man in the gutter, though not sunk yet, I was low.

Another gale, then the wind went back to the south-west and the sun reappeared. Even after only a short time it is amazing how a little burst of sun can restore spirits. During the following morning, a speck crossed the horizon but disappeared quickly, having raised my hopes of a ship only to be disappointed. Overhead I saw the vapour trails of jet aircraft. Clearly the *Kilcullen* was now close, if not on the main shipping lanes. Up above, I marvelled and speculated what was going on in the jet. An air hostess was probably serving somebody a fresh cup of coffee while in a very short time all of her passengers would be home with their families having crossed the Atlantic in a matter of hours, while it was taking the *Kilcullen* two months. There would probably be a pin-striped Englishman, an Arab sheikh or even an American millionaire in the first-class cabin—if only I had accepted that kind offer of a seat home from John Hutchins in Annapolis, months before!

Of course being on the shipping lanes was no guarantee that I would encounter a ship or, if I did, that a ship would see the *Kilcullen* and stop and stock up my larder. But there was hope. While aircraft follow the lanes strictly, principally taking the shortest Great-Circle route, ships invariably become much more spread out. Each day passed but still no luck. I began to despair and had flares constantly at the ready should a ship come into view within any sort of reasonable distance. Soon the storms commonly associated with the equinox were to be expected and, above all else, I needed food to give me the physical and psychological strength to fight them.

The morning of September 7th was crisp, the rising sun through the clear sky sparkled on the flat, windless ocean. A small speck appeared on the horizon and gradually grew bigger. At first I thought it a fishing boat but no, it grew and grew into a massive oil tanker. Would she see me? Would they speak English?

'Yippee!' I roared. She was coming straight on the *Kilcullen*'s path. I ignited some hand flares but there was no need, clearly the ship had altered course, started to circle, and was slowing down.

'Food, food!' I roared, though they were still clearly too far away. There was a flurry of activity on the deck as bodies—real people—moved up and down. Manning the oars, it seemed to take me forever before I got alongside the gigantic orange-painted ship. I grabbed on to a thick, greasy rope the ship had dropped over the side: though the ocean seemed calm, it was risky sliding up and down the towering sides of the giant tanker. I stared up at the crew as they stared down on me.

'Good morning,' a voice bellowed down at me. It was strange to hear another human voice after so long.

'It's great to see you, can you give me a supply of food?'

'We'll send a ladder down and you can climb on board,' the voice replied, clearly that of an English officer. 'Where have you come from in that thing, we'll take you from here.'

'No, no,' was my instant response, explaining that the *Kilcullen* had departed Halifax nearly forty days previously. I also asked again for some supplies and said that it would be unsafe for me to climb on board.

Strange as this may seem, I was only alongside the ship called the *Post Champion* for a few minutes and already I wanted to get away. She was out of London and, going the other way, bound for New York, one of the last places in the world I wanted to go to at that point.

The crew kindly gathered a great big bag of all sorts of provisions, a welcome sight indeed, and passed it down along the rope. While this was happening, I was terrified by the surging swell up and down the side of the tanker, while an early morning conversation continued with several of the crew members.

'My inflatable is called the *Kilcullen,* I'm bound for Kilronan in the Aran Islands. Can you please report my position?' This the captain kindly did. Again I was unaware that so many ashore were concerned for the safety of the *Kilcullen* at that stage; frankly I did not want them to be, nor did I feel that I was worth being concerned about.

Just before I departed from the *Post Champion* into the isolation once again, the mate roared out from the ship's bridge: 'Er, er...would you like to check your position, sir?' in a posh accent. By the way he spoke I could not helping getting the feeling that in his reserved British humour, he was taking the micky out of the Irishman they had just found in the rubber dinghy.

'Sure, where am I?' I replied in my best Galway accent. It had been foolish of me not to ask for a position check before this, and the mate's gesture was appreciated.

After a few moments he returned and bellowed out, as only a ship's officer can, backed by years of experience blasting orders from the bridge. 'Your position is 43 degrees 35 North and 26 degrees West!'

Strange, I thought. This position would put the *Kilcullen* much further south than I thought, about 180 miles off course. Then somewhat reluctantly, I queried his position and asked him to check again. I did feel it was a bit brazen of me in the tiny *Kilcullen* to question the position of an ocean-going tanker—the mate had such an air of authority.

'Perhaps the latitude is around 46 degrees and not 43 degrees North,' I said.

After checking, to his surprise and embarrassment, the mate had to confirm that he had given the wrong position: the ship's navigation was not wrong, but a six had been read off as a three. Meanwhile, many of the crew, looking over the side and hanging on every word, were very much amused. 'Thanks very much for the assistance in navigation,' one of them said as we parted company. 'Any time, feel free!' said I, pleased as Punch.

Then, with friendly greetings, good luck wishes and laughter, the *Post Champion* was gone, disappearing as she had come, a speck on the horizon. I was happy to be alone again, happier still with a fresh supply of food and a position check. There were now less than 700 miles to go; having been through so much, I would let nothing stop us now.

It is only on reflection back that I have come to realize the psychological consequences, had I not been cheeky in asking the mate to check his position. After so long with nothing but sun sights, navigational tables and hundreds of calculations, had the position the *Post Champion* gave me been correct, my own calculations up to that point and, ultimately, my mind would have been thrown into total confusion.

In many respects I regarded the *Post Champion* as an intrusion on the private little world of the *Kilcullen,* though the supplies were a very welcome intrusion indeed. Content and happy, as the wind filled in once again with a chill to it. I no longer saw my isolation as a thing to be feared, but more a cherished companion, without whom I was at a loss.

10

So close, yet so far

AT THIS stage I started to give serious consideration to a landfall. For this precise navigation would be important and it would be stupid to get mashed up on the rugged western seaboard of Ireland, having voyaged 3,000 miles. Happily, with plenty of food and good sunlight, we got some good positions and the distance home kept diminishing.

At least there was the outboard motor with a supply of petrol saved for the landfall. I had kept it well sealed in a plastic bag, so I thought, but I decided to check, I attempted to start the motor but there was no way she would even give a spark—the electrics under the flywheel had seized. This was maddening; having brought the motor all this way, I now could not use it. In reality I should have protected it better and given it a run now and then, this would have been easy when the seas were flat.

At least the transistor radio was working and European radio stations started to come in at night. Then Irish radio came in: 'Armed men got away with a large sum of money after robbing the Sligo mail train this evening . . . The hospital maintenance men's strike continues.' These two headlines, read by Maurice O'Doherty, made me jump for joy. They were still robbing banks and going on strike, nothing had changed in Ireland since I left it eighteen months previously.

Now a strong south westerly wind set in. It was perfect for the *Kilcullen*'s course, pointed on the south-west corner of Ireland. The calculated gamble of staying well south, in anticipation of this south-westerly, was starting to pay off. It blew steady for almost 36 hours and I covered a near record 140 miles with all sail up.

Visions of a disastrous landfall kept returning. And then the pleasures: walking on solid land that did not move, sitting in an armchair, enjoying a pint of Guinness and a soft bed.

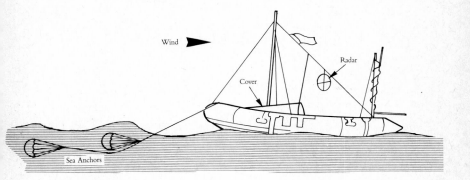

The wind put out the timetable; it veered from south-west to north-east. For two days, I lay at sea-anchor waiting for it to change. Though not blowing strongly, it held me back. At this rate it would be another month, not a week as I thought, before I made my landfall. I jumped up and down, screamed and shadow-boxed the cruel contrary wind. 'This is stupid, this is unfair, give us a break,' I roared, but to no avail. It was getting colder and colder, and I resorted to at least four layers of clothes to stay warm. Everything was damp in the salt air and the constant salt sores were a source of irritation.

Going to the toilet was again a problem as I cursed the small bucket. Then one evening, just after emptying the bucket over the side with my droppings, a shark swiftly came and gobbled up the contents. It was a lone blue shark, some twelve feet in length and had been following the *Kilcullen* for some days now. I had first noticed him going over and back, scraping his backside off the *Kilcullen*'s bottom. Later I concluded that he must have been scraping some sort of parasite worms on his back. Being a stationary object, lying to a sea-anchor, the *Kilcullen* was an attraction. When the shark first started scraping himself on the *Kilcullen* I was scared out of my wits, till I had the bright idea of putting down the long white shaft of the outboard motor and he started scraping himself on this instead.

Eventually the shark, which I christened Easter, became a regular visitor and he no longer scared me; I even had a go at taking a photograph of him with a waterproof camera. Each time Easter's fin passed under the stern he was so close that I felt like patting him, like a man would do to his dog. However, since he might have snapped off my hand, I resisted the impulse.

The Nor' easterly abated, the wind swung west and, spirits restored, the *Kilcullen* got moving again. I'd not seen Easter for some time until one evening I ate a can of sardines and, without thinking, threw the empty can overboard. Within seconds, Easter was alongside, looking for more once he got a sniff of the sardine oil in the dregs of the can. There is little these creatures miss in their kingdom of the sea.

With each remaining day I was becoming more and more on edge, and my sleep interrupted by the slightest change in the *Kilcullen*'s movement. One of the air compartments had gone completely flat and, while the boat was not in danger of sinking, the water did now wash over the side and could give me serious problems. There was no indication as to how the compartment had gone flat. I feared a hole outside below the waterline which would be virtually impossible to fix. Inch by inch, I started a careful investigation to find the hole.

Eventually, working under a constant drizzle, I found the hole, inside the dinghy but in an awkward position to patch. Apparently a rough edge on the dislocated floorboard, from the time the *Kilcullen* fell off the wave, had done it. At least the flat compartment made it easier to remove the board and fix a patch which, after some difficulty, made a seal.

The wind now drew further east and increased to gale force and it was no longer possible for me to hold course. The seas were starting to build and the only alternative to being blown backwards was to lie to a sea anchor—again. The date was September 13th and the *Kilcullen*'s dead reckoning position was 51° 45' N., 18° 50'W., only 350 miles south and west of Galway.

There was nothing for it but to sit and wait. I lay huddled under the canvas cover and wet sleeping bag, but I had been through it all before and just had to ride it out. As long as the sea anchors held at least I should be stable enough.

Two sea-anchors and their securing lines did break away but, I managed to secure two spare ones from the bow. Trembling, after the job was done, back under the cover in the half light I felt afraid. The sea was in a furious humour; every so often a very big wave would come surging forward, its thundering roar distinguishing it from the rest, until it would break—covering the dinghy in a mass of water. Each time a quantity of this salty cold sea would leak through the canopy, sometimes running down my neck or back—giving me a cold shiver down my spine.

By September 16th the storm had eased and the sun made a brave, reassuring appearance through the fast moving clouds that raced overhead. It looked as if the worst had passed but no, it was only a temporary reprieve, soon the storm returned with all its fury, this time from the north-east.

'Wait, wait, be patient, do not do anything irrational, we can weather and beat it all,' I kept telling myself and stroked the side tubes affectionately; even if only a chunk of rubber, the *Kilcullen* would see me through. At least the terns were confident as they bobbed up and down quite happily, oblivious to my plight. How these little creatures survive, hundreds of miles from land, in storms like this—it makes one think!

Daylight on the 17th brought bright sunlight and improved spirits. Clearly the worst was over, but the seas were still enormous having built over four days. Another night came and, like an ostrich with his head in the sand, I huddled helplessly under the cover of a wet sleeping bag. It is more the sound of the waves that haunt my mind than seeing them head on. Over the living area of some ten feet, much of the *Kilcullen*'s gear and equipment was spread in disorder. In previous storms I would have had it all lashed together but now, having come through so much, I had all too much confidence in the *Kilcullen*. She had beaten this storm, like all the rest, she was without question the unsinkable, pneumatic lady of the sea.

In the early morning light I lay half awake under the cover. All the sounds of the sea indicated that the storm had blown itself out. It would now be only a matter of time before conditions eased and we could be on our merry way once again.

I vividly remember a cracking sound and a snap forward. 'Must be the damn sea-anchor line breaking again,' I thought. 'Ah, sure it can wait. The sun will be warming up soon and the storm is easing. What difference is another few miles backwards

going to make? Sure, I'm lovely and cozy here.'

At first it was just an ordinary breaking wave but the sound kept getting louder. Then it became an almighty roar, one which I will never forget. There was a great thud, clatter, crashing, crunch.

Next I was looking into the ocean. Everything had gone crazy in an upside down world. I gasped for air and kicked in the tangled web to get clear of the sleeping bag.

11

World upside down

IT WAS a pocket of air trapped under the *Kilcullen* which gave me a temporary reprieve as I kicked and struggled to get clear of the water-logged sleeping bag dragging me down.

The old head was going crazy; keep calm, keep calm, I kept saying to myself as what seemed like a million thoughts flashed through the brain. It is true when they say that at a time of crisis your entire life rushes past in seconds. Every fear I had ever nourished was now raw, not least being the hope that Easter, the shark, was not around.

Swiftly the cold of the ocean started to penetrate as I dived down and up round the side of the *Kilcullen*. Then it was a struggle to climb on the up-turned bottom to join the slimy growth and barnacles—shocked as I was at the sudden exposure and the topsy turvy state of affairs. Immediately the cold biting wind pierced through the T-shirt and trousers I had on, for I had kicked off my other clothes to swim. Already my feet were numb and could hardly be moved. Quickly I started to rub them in order to get circulation going. This was terrifying: if I was like this after five minutes, what chance had I of surviving? Frostbite and exposure would strike before there was time to drown.

As each wave came pounding over, making it difficult to hold a grip, and the boat's gear was being quickly washed away, it was critical to act fast. Initially the canvas cover had saved me from being thrown into the sea and lost on capsize; likewise it had trapped much of the equipment and stores, but that would not be for long.

It must have been around six in the morning, just as it was

starting to get light. Everything was grey, grim, and the sky looked angry. Overhead some great big seagulls hovered around like vultures, completely indifferent to the *Kilcullen*'s plight. Other gulls bobbed up and down in the lee of the dinghy as before, taking advantage of the little shelter offered. I only realized the size of the birds when later they became more daring and landed almost beside me. The weed-growth, and upturned barnacles were fresh food to them here, over 200 miles from the nearest land.

After several quick dives back under the boat I saved the survival suit, radio beacon, flares, survival rations, sleeping bag and other bits and pieces of equipment, in that order of importance. After the initial shock and cold, the numbness was now not so bad as circulation returned. But each dive was a struggle, risky and exhausting. Between swims and spurts of action I would huddle up on the bottom for a few minutes to get some warmth and conserve energy.

Even gear I had saved was being washed away with the breaking seas. No sooner had I something lashed when it worked loose again. Once gone from its haphazard lashing, the surging swell would carry it away fast out of sight. This happened to the last remaining water container—luckily I saw it drifting away: without water my survival chances were slimmer. There was not a second to spare as I dived into the cold sea after the container, nor was there time to rig a safety line.

Getting back to the boat with the container was the struggle of a lifetime. I swam a sort of bastardised side-stroke, holding the container; it was one stroke backwards for every two forward - sometimes backwards altogether. As I struggled back to the dinghy I really began to doubt whether I'd make it this time, but the animal instinct proved strong, and strength came from nothing. I crawled back on to the bottom, exhausted.

For a long time I just hung on, drained of energy and at one stage shouting: 'You silly fool, you were overconfident and now look ...' There had been two plans to right the *Kilcullen* in the event of a capsize. Neither worked. The first involved lifting one side out of the water with empty water and fuel bags while standing on the other side with a rope. The second involved deflating the tubes on one side: this would have eventually worked had three of the five tubes been deflated, but under the circumstances I decide that it was too risky and adopted a survival mode instead in the hope of rescue.

What now? The first day was almost over by the time everything was secured. Yet still the waves kept washing things away, including the O'Coineen carcass which I lashed to the bottom. By comparison, my situation just 24 hours previously looked like heaven and I wished that I could go back in time.

How long could I survive like this? Being north of the shipping lanes the chance of being sighted were slim. The only hope lay in the emergency position-indicator beacon which, with limited battery power, I switched on and off from time to time. Closely I hugged, talked to and kissed this little radio. Like never before I prayed and asked God to help and for strength to survive.

Why had *Kilcullen* capsized? Alright, so I had miscalculated and been lulled and over-confident. But still, what had caused it now and never before? Evidently the sea-anchors had snapped and, in my delay in getting up, the *Kilcullen* lay sideways and was flipped by a rogue wave. I'm glad I didn't see the bastard but its roar haunts me like a nightmare. If only this and if only that . . .

That first night crawled like a slow snail. Alone with every thought in the world, it was hard to accept the seriousness of the position. Though the storm had eased, the seas were still big and there was no alternative but to wait and conserve energy. Every so often during the darkness a wave would come crashing, breaking over the entire dinghy, covering me with the icy sea which ran down my back. Twice I was washed overboard, to scramble back each time by the lashing line.

Dawn of the following morning brought an increase in temperature and my spirits improved slightly. But there was still no sign of a ship as I scanned the horizon with flares on the ready. If the wind went around to the west, as it should do eventually, it would be two weeks of drifting before a landfall could be hoped for. There was nothing to do but nibble at the survival rations and water supply and wait. It was just grim, grey and overcast as I remained alone with my thoughts. By evening the wind had started to increase again and, as darkness closed in, I wondered would I ever see the light of day again.

I re-lashed my body on the lines which kept working loose. It was cold. I was afraid to go asleep in case I didn't wake up, it was also important to keep a look-out for the lights of ships. While holding the emergency radio beacon as high as possible between my arms, every so often I would doze off.

Death was staring me in the face. Again there was little of my life that I did not think of. Childhood and many long-forgotten memories returned clearly. There was a great need to tell people at home and friends that there was no cause of concern. This was entirely my own undertaking and risk, now the consequences must be accepted. I did not want to die but I wanted everybody to know that I had fought to the very end and tried everything to stay alive.

There was another dark side to my nature which emerged. It is downright curiosity and I wondered what it would be like to be dead. Death must be the ultimate adventure and once-off kick.

Now the consequences of not making it were very real. Up until now it had in many ways been a boy's game. The radio beacon did not seem to be doing its job. It must surely be the end. What was death really like? How would it happen? Was it like falling asleep? Was it the start of a new adventure? If so I was anxious to get on with it and give it a try. Certainly the world would not miss Enda. Millions would take my place. I was now, I thought, on the way to other things which could not be any worse than this. The intense cold was now right through to the bones and my body seemed to be slipping from me.

We must all bow to the inevitable, but it must be a fight to the very end. Fate is fate. What will happen will happen. Life had been good, there would be no regrets. I also tried to pray because this is what you are supposed to do at a time like this, but I soon gave up. There must be a God of sorts, there must be some powerful force, but I'm damned if I know what it is.

And still the seas kept pounding. There was no moon or stars; they were all hidden by the turbulent fast moving clouds. The night was black but, like the grass must grow, dawn had to come and I knew that if I made it to that point I would live for another day.

Oh for bright warm sunshine, oh to be miles from here on a tropical beach in the West Indies alongside a black girl tickling me with a feather—Absurd!—Oh for this, oh for that, who cares?

It was half dawn. First there was a rumbling sound in the

distance. First I thought it to be thunder but then it got louder and louder. Was it a plane, a jet? Would it see the *Kilcullen?* Like crazy, coming out of a daze, I fumbled for the bag of flares. It was a low-flying jet. Now he almost flew right over the *Kilcullen* but seemed to continue on. 'Was it too late?' I thought as I ignited precious parachute flares, nearly burning myself alive in the process, and lighting up the sky like Hallowe'en.

Since I was a dark object low down at sea level, there was little chance that the pilot would see such a dot on the ocean, though he might know I was in the area. My heart sunk as gradually the sound of the jet became quieter. I was in despair until the sound returned again, getting louder and louder; this time I was ready with the flares. The jet replied with a green rocket. Spotted at last!

Spotted yes, but how long till rescue? It could take days to divert a ship to pick up the *Kilcullen*. Several times the aircraft, which turned out to be an RAF Nimrod from Scotland, flew over and back. I felt mighty grateful that they were taking such an interest but embarassed at all the attention and the cost of the fuel for the jet. This situation was my own doing and I imagined a little man constantly pouring petrol into the gigantic jet engines at a gallon a minute.

By this time the wind was raging again and the waves building up, as I watched the Nimrod, like a World War II bomber, open hatches on her belly and drop objects into the ocean, falling at first like bombs, upwind of the *Kilcullen*. Well, they weren't bombs, but it was not immediately clear to me that they were liferafts. Two in fact: one landed miles away and the other landed quite close upwind. It had inflated automatically but was upside down. Though reluctant to leave the relative security of the *Kilcullen*, I swam towards the raft. The righting instructions were very clearly written on the bottom; I climbed aboard in an exhausted and hungry state. Unfortunately I could not get the container with provisions open.

Everything about the liferaft was flimsy. Since it had not inflated fully it was not as comfortable or secure as it should have been and in a short time, with the change of movement and bouncing of the raft, I became violently seasick—a condition which seemed absurd after so long at sea. Having no food to puke up added to the agony. However I managed to lash the

Kilcullen to the liferaft in an effort to save her and maintain the vain hope of a landfall. I was on my own once more on the wide, tumbling sea.

Five hours later (we were now well into the morning of September 19th), I heard the rumbling of engines and looked up to see a large ship, growing larger every minute. There were voices, excitement, rows of oriental faces lining the bulwarks and orders flying in all directions. Within minutes I was sitting in a hot bath tub, holding a glass of brandy.

'There don't seem to be any physical defects,' I heard Commander Bawtree say to the captain on the ship's phone. 'He seems to have mild exposure, nothing that heat, plenty of rest and nourishment cannot cure.'

I was gripped with a peculiar fear, a fear of meeting people again and explaining myself. Had I gone strange, what would their reaction be to me? The brandy made me light-headed and helped me not to worry. Others had taken charge of me— decisions were no longer in my hands.

'You're on board the *Stromness,* A Royal Navy supply ship,' Commander Bawtree told me. He was the ship's surgeon, and the ship, he explained, was on its way to Norfolk, Virginia. A kind, sensitive man with a sense of humour, the surgeon explained the presence of so many oriental faces on board a Royal Fleet Auxiliary ship. 'We were stationed in Hong Kong for some time, and these people do such a bloody good job you know.'

He gave orders that the survivor was not to be disturbed, though, within a short period the curious and friendly Chinese crew were slipping into the sick bay with gifts of fruit and cigarettes.

Next Captain Stanley arrived in person. He too was bubbling over with curiosity but he managed to conceal this in a more reserved manner.

After thanking him most heartily for rescuing me, I told him that I was so close to home and would rather not be whisked back across the Atlantic. I'd done enough travelling. 'Is there any way, sir, that you can drop me off close to Ireland for a landfall?' I asked. 'No need to land me in Ireland—just a question of blowing up the *Kilcullen* again and leaving me in it with a few stores.'

Politely he replied that this was not a good idea, though I

suspect he thought me quite mad, having only just been plucked out of the stormy ocean. He brooded for a while, then his face brightened. 'We're expecting to rendezvous shortly,' he said, with a Royal Navy destroyer on a NATO exercise off the west coast of Ireland. 'Maybe we can transfer you . . .' And so it came to pass.

Both the destroyer and the *Stromness* sailed at fifteen knots into the wind on a computer-linked course. The *Kilcullen* and I were transferred on a cable secured between the two ships. The seas were still enormous as the two ships crashed through the waves, spraying fountains of water up the slot between their hulls. As a naval exercise it was an impressive business, demanding great precision and co-ordination and the actual transfer was a nerve-racking affair.

The pending arrival of a castaway by the name of Enda on the all-male destroyer caused consternation. Enda became Edna and a woman was expected on this war ship, very much a man's world. Sailors amused themselves by putting 'Ladies' signs on the heads, there were searches for articles of clothing and the men took bets on the lady's looks and vital statistics. Needless to say I was a big disappointment, though the rumour, once started, could not be dispelled and filtered right back to the mainland where for a time, it was thought that there were actually two survivors.

I expected to bunk down with the deck hands and join them in their Mess, so imagine my surprise when I was shown into a cabin in Officers' Row: it was a visiting captain's sea cabin. As I was a skipper myself, albeit of a leaky rubber boat, I was given VIP treatment, as naval etiquette required. I had the run of the ship and was extremely well looked after. Dressed in an officer's trousers and shirt, without the badges, I dined that evening in the officers' ward room, under a portrait of H.M. the Queen and the Duke of Edinburgh. What a change from 24 hours ago, when I was trying not to get swept off my upturned dinghy!

'Jolly good, great to have you aboard old chap,' they all told me. Inevitably they were amused and, in their own polite way took the Mickey out of the Irishman found in the rubber dinghy. Still, I was in good spirits and kept my end up. Besides, they were a fantastic bunch, very friendly and hospitable, and as seamen they understood the adventure pefectly well.

At sea for over six weeks, the diversion on the destroyer *Ambuscade* was welcome. As part of the NATO war fleet we were participating in so-called top secret manoeuvres off the west coast of Ireland and Scotland. War games for just in case—as long as they remained only games!

One officer gave me a log book to start recording details of the *Kilcullen* voyage while it remained fresh in my mind. That's one of the best things I've ever been given, for it has made a relatively accurate account of the whole thing from start to finish possible.

Meanwhile news of the *Kilcullen* adventure had leaked out to the world and the media had made a meal of it. The rescue operation turned out to be a very good public relations exercise for the Royal Navy, and I was glad to play my part. Their ocean rescue activities perform such a good and necessary role that I shall be forever indebted to them. Happily I was at sea and cut off from all the excitement generated. But the stories that got around about me grew more fantastic with the telling. I heard of one report, for instance, in a Spanish newspaper, which spoke about an Irishman found by the British in the middle of the Atlantic drinking Guinness and on the verge of madness in an inflatable canoe.

In no time at all, though about a stone lighter, I was back to my old self. The food was excellent and I was waited on hand and foot—like a true officer. The entire NATO fleet was due to arrive in England together, while I still entertained thoughts of being dropped off in the *Kilcullen* to make my own landfall. Though much gear was lost, the *Kilcullen* was airtight and looked in reasonable order. The only thing was, could I persuade the captain?

He listened carefully. For over an hour we discussed it and argued. 'You'll have no worries, everything will be OK. I'll have to get back home anyway,' I explained. Surely he could simply let the *Kilcullen* off close to land, if not back where I was picked up, to make the ultimate landfall. The captain said that he quite understood but the decision did not rest with him. The request was passed on to the fleet commodore, a Dutchman, whose ship was steaming close by.

The commodore could not make the decision either, so he radioed the request to his superiors, at NATO fleet headquarters near London. However, the NATO men deliberated and came back with an emphatic no—things looked very different ashore. I was very upset over this at the time but in retrospect, I can see that they would have looked a bit silly (and so would I) if they had had to rescue the *Kilcullen* a second time!

In fact the commodore flew over on his helicopter to the *Ambuscade* to see me personally. He invited me to fly back to his ship so that I could sit beside him for the press conference when the NATO fleet arrived in Plymouth. I thanked him kindly but preferred to stay in the *Ambuscade* with the *Kilcullen*. With the frigate's last few days at sea after a six-month stint I was conscious as never before of the great comradeship among the crew and of the way they drew the singlehanded survivor into their company. During the last night before docking many dressed up in fancy dress, and there was a sod's opera with some very original skits—one on Paddy the Irishman they found in the inflatable.

I landed at Plymouth on Monday, September 26th, eleven days after being plucked out of the sea. The world's media were less interested in meeting the Dutch commodore at the press conference than in seeing the survivor. They turned up in a mob to meet me on board *Ambuscade*. I had never been the centre of such attention and found it a curious experience. A lady from the BBC called Angela Rippon, whom I had never heard of, interviewed me. (It was at the time that her legs controversy was at its height, so this all caused quite a stir with the sailors.) I told her about the careful preparations for the voyage and about Murphy's Law; this she asked me to explain. And so it came to pass that the young survivor told the British public in their homes that evening all about Murphy's Law.

After an interview with a *Daily Express* reporter, John Burns of Belfast, who gave me £600 in hard cash, I managed to clear Customs and Immigration with the inflatable and make for the railway station. My plan was to travel by British Rail to Holyhead, reinflate the *Kilcullen,* and wait for a favourable weather window to make for Dublin.

At Plymouth there was nobody to meet me from my part of Ireland and, suddenly, I was very much alone again—though there were lots of people around. Travelling with a transatlantic yacht through England, making the various rail connections, was an adventure in itself. Going through some suburban areas and making rush hour connections, bumping into men with umbrellas and leather cases, represented the complete contrast. In total, British Rail, bless its heart, charged me an extra £1-50 for excess baggage.

A good friend and cousin, Brian Lynch, arrived from Galway to try unsuccessfully to persuade me not to make the Irish Sea crossing, but I still had my heart set on stepping ashore from the *Kilcullen,* and after a long wait for the weather to improve, on 3 October 1977, the *Kilcullen* made her final landfall in Dun Laoghaire. It was a damp Monday morning. After demolishing a pint of black porter I got a lift to cousin Eamon and Renee Lynch's house in suburbia. Then, lo and behold, when soaking naked in a hot bath, the Irish press finally caught up with me. They were anxious to make their evening edition deadlines so I talked to them from the tub—effectively a press conference from the bath. Dear Mother, back at home, was understandably shocked to see my nakedness, hidden only by the bathwater, boldly exposed in the following morning's papers.

That was it. In all sincerity I vowed: 'Never again.' However, I had yet to learn that 'never' is a word one has to do without.

12

Down and out

READJUSTMENT back to normal life was a difficult process, and you may well enquire: what is normal? Swiftly I learned that your name may have been splashed all over the papers, you may be a hero of sorts, but all that matters is what you achieve within your own spirit.

Having lost a great deal of weight, it did not take me long to get back into shape physically, but for my mental faculties it was a longer haul. People might stop me on country lanes if they recognized my face, but it would not be to ask for my autograph—rather to point me out to their friends as a prodigy of reckless lunacy.

Nor did the publicity help get a job, quite the contrary, in many respects it made me unemployable. By coming so far on the inflatable and eventually getting home I had always felt that I had achieved in many respects what I had set out to do, but in the eyes of the world I had been over-ambitious and fallen flat on my face. A miss is as good as a mile.

In cash terms, I ended with IR£1,000 in my pocket, repre-senting the proceeds from newspaper articles. This was a fortune, or so it seemed at the time. Having nurtured three simple ambitions—to own a grandfather clock, a tandem bicycle and a Morris Minor—I went out and bought the latter. I called her Betsy, like my other old faithful, but we were not destined to remain partners for long. Driving home two weeks later from giving a lecture to the University Sailing Club in Galway—one I had helped to found—I had had a beer too many and have to confess that, as the judge would say, I was unfit through drink. As I drove through the town at night, the road turned right but Betsy and I kept on going. A steel telegraph pole and a concrete wall stopped us. How we both suffered!

The young doctor on Casualty stopped the bleeding, removed the glass from my head, and stitched it up with a small scar remaining under my hair to the present day. Unfortunately I had no tax or insurance and the car had four bald tyres and a ropy suspension so, not surprisingly, the Garda, having arrived on the scene of the accident after I had left, came looking in the hospital.

'Where is the victim?' I heard them enquire outside the casualty room.

'He's o.k. Nothing too serious, but he needs rest and should not be disturbed,' the doctor replied. As luck would have it, I had known him in college as a student.

I got out of the hospital with a big bandage around my head, 'a ghastly sight,' I was told afterwards by the motor mechanic whom I had got up out of bed.

'What in the thunderin' name of Jesus do you want at this hour of the morning?' he roared from the top window of his three-bedroomed suburban home.

'The car, the car . . . 'tis crashed, we must get it away before the Garda examine it,' said I, anxious that none of the defects be found.

'O.K., O.K.,' my friend replied, while muttering that I'd be better off out in the middle of the Atlantic. He told me to get out of his house and go to bed. Later he informed me that he got the car away to the scrapyard just ahead of the Garda. At the end of the day the evidence had gone and he had collected £40 from the scrapdealer . . . End of car and end of story. In truth, I deserved to be caught but got away scot free. Now with age, my attitude to motoring is a lot more responsible. I still don't have a tandem bicycle and do not have a place suitable to keep a grandfather clock, but the day will come . . .

More by accident than design, I ended up working as a journalist. It started when, by chance, I met Tim Pat Coogan, the editor of The Irish Press newspaper, who had the paper make me an offer to write a weekly column about boats. At that time, I didn't even know what a newspaper column was—not least what it involved to write one. Fortunately I said yes and learned fast, and the column thrived. I also got a start with a new boating magazine and though at many times in a semi-perpetual state of confused disorganization, I learned a great deal fast.

All of this involved moving across Ireland to live in Dublin. People talk about the isolation and loneliness of the Atlantic but, for that first period in the big city with thousands of people around, I was never so alone. In time new friends emerged and I was able to renew my leisure-time interest in sailing while the more formal yachting establishment of Dun Laoghaire took some getting used to.

Time raced forward. While the inflatable Atlantic affair drifted further into the past, it kept resurfacing in the most peculiar ways. One time, an enthusiastic priest invited me to open a festival in Clare on the Atlantic seaboard. He had read my articles and determined that this adventurer would be perfect to inject a little enthusiasm into the local community because I had almost made it.

There were only two pubs. The rain poured down unremittingly while the weather was too wild for my proposed landing on the beach in a currach to open the festival. Instead, behind an Irish band blaring away out of tune, I marched. With two currach oars overhead, we went up and down the town several times, my presence being more a joke than anything else. Being a celebrity in rural Ireland, I discovered, is just not the done thing.

Eventually the groaning band drummed enough enthusiasm to get some of the people out of the pubs for the official opening. This involved me standing on hay, made to look like a boat, beside a barrel. Then there was a rope tied to a rock (which was to be an anchor but none could be found) my one act being to throw the rock, cast the anchor and declare the festival open. Then everybody returned to the pubs to get on with the real festival.

Feeling like a fish out of water, I got a lift to the main road as quick as possible and hitched a ride back to Dublin suburbia while promising myself never again. This sort of carry-on may be O.K. for actors and older people but for somebody still in their early twenties, festival opening is something to be avoided like the plague.

A festival of another extreme I got involved in was that of Cowes Week, which every second year sees the start of the Fastnet Race. A focal point for royalty, high society and yachters. It was 1979 and I found myself crewing on board Brian Kelly's *Rapparee,* a Shamrock half-tonner out of Howth and, at 29 feet, one of the smallest yachts in the race. That was the race in which fifteen people were to be drowned and the sporting world quite shaken.

13

Fastnet Storms

IT WAS A blustery Saturday in August. On the Cowes, Isle of Wight sea front, the breeze set the pennants cracking at the mast-heads, and lifted the fashionable ladies' hats—when it did not lift their skirts. Some 300 yachts approached the starting line in an atmosphere of great tension at the start of a gruelling 604-mile race to the Fastnet Rock, a few miles off south-west Ireland, and back. The yachts varied in size from 29 feet to 90 feet approximately. Somewhere in the middle of it all I was there on board *Rapparee,* fully loaded and prepared for a week's keen racing.

First there was white gun-smoke, followed seconds later by the blast of the Royal Yacht Squadron cannon. Its reverbations ripped across the starting line and we were off. To be at sea again, this time with a good crew, was pleasure indeed—to be breathing the fresh sea air through flying spray and ripping through the waves. Not really the *Kilcullen*'s scene. The Fastner's recent history had been one of light winds, and many crews were not adequately prepared for the conditions we were to encounter. One of our crew, for instance, was a bank clerk, and he arrived on board with suntan oil, Bermuda shorts, sunglasses, and a guide to Irish income tax. Later his book was fished out from the bilge as a mass of paper pulp.

After the starting gun, we raced up the Solent towards the open sea and English Channel with 79 entries in our group, we constantly crossed each other in tacking duels.

'Ready about, let go genny ... Lee ho! ... Main coming across, watch your heads.' *Rapparee* trundled along in the 15-knot headwind. Then it was not long before the sleek thoroughbred ocean racers from the Admiral's cup fleet, which started after us, overtook us. In all, over 2,000 yachtsmen were racing towards the Fastnet rock.

Soon we had cleared the excitement of the start, the fleet scattered and darkness approached. With so much traffic, a constant lookout was essential as the wind remained on the nose. Dawn brought some relief as the fleet made for Land's End, the south-west tip of England. And while the wind remained moderate the atmosphere felt uncannily tense—there was something brewing but nobody knew quite what. One hint was a long rolling swell coming in from the south-west, but seemingly there was no wind. It was an indication, though, of strong winds in the offing. Meanwhile, out in the Atlantic the forecasters spoke of a low-pressure system moving at 45 knots, no sluggard.

However, the buzz around the fleet was that the low would wash harmlessly by. Ashore, the experts were predicting that the 1979 Fastnet would suffer from slack winds and no records would be broken. That was before the storm struck the fleet.

'Quick, get the genny down,' the skipper ordered; but it wouldn't come, preferring to remain snagged up the mast. So I had to climb the mast and cut down the expensive new, lightweight sail. Rolling around as much as forty degrees either side was no joke thirty feet in the air, and I was extremely nervous, but the job had to be done.

That Monday night the wind increased even more. We had no warning though Kevin had suggested that the barometer needle was dropping so fast that we use a match stick to prop it up. By the time the so-called weather experts ashore had realized what was happening with the depression, now named Low Y, it was too late for insertion in the forecast.

The seas had started to build rapidly. In no time we were down to a storm jib, with nothing else driving *Rapparee* along. It was a striking contrast to the almost flat calm of the previous night off the Lizard. The big waves were close together and no sooner had the bow burst free to ride one wall of water than the next would come crashing down.

First we tried running off before the storm but *Rapparee* was pounding furiously and moving too fast, despite trailing warps behind—a classic textbook manner to ride a storm. But *Rapparee* had never been in a storm like this before and she virtually told us what to do: lie a-hull. This involved dropping the storm jib completely and lashing the helm over, leaving the boat to its own devices while the crew remained sealed below decks.

But this was not before a mountain of a wave knocked *Rappa-ree* over and completely swamped the cockpit, taking two crew members overboard. Fortunately, by the grace of God, we got them back again, saved by their safety harnesses which held firm. Below decks the cooker had broken loose and at one stage was practically sitting on the deckhead. We spent the night mopping up without a great deal of optimism and waiting for better weather. How the rest of the fleet were faring we had no idea— our radio had gone for a ride.

Grimalkin, a yacht similar to ours, was nearby. They ran off before the storm under storm jib, trailing warps. All six crewmen remained huddled in the cockpit together for company and warmth. The yacht was knocked down several times and, though their craft remained afloat, the crew became exhausted and dispirited from being on deck all the time. One crewman's lifeline broke and he was washed away. After many more knockdowns the boat became a shambles and the remaining crew decided to send out a Mayday distress signal and take to the liferaft.

Three made it to the liferaft before it was separated from the yacht while the other two were given up for dead. The liferaft group were winched up by a helicopter and much to everybody's surprise, one of the crewmen who had been left for dead later recovered and was picked up by the same helicopter. *Grimalkin* survived the storm almost intact, and was later towed to Waterford.

Luckily, *Grimalkin*'s liferaft group were picked up quickly. Many more crews who had taken to liferafts were lost as the liferafts broke up. In truth you cannot expect a light inflatable craft to stand up to the elements when a regular craft cannot. The great moral to this story is to stay with your craft and stay below decks to conserve energy and strength in a storm.

Though few storms are the same, had I been alone on board my 16ft inflatable boat *Kilcullen*, I am convinced that she would not have broken up like the other liferafts. Of course the *Kilcullen* was designed as a boat and, when all else fails, an inflatable dinghy that doubles as a liferaft with a CO_2 cylinder for quick inflation and other safety gear is in my view a much better bet.

Many yachts around *Rapparee* suffered disaster as winds accelerated to sixty knots and took the top off the ocean. We were still on the Continental Shelf in relatively shallow water in the vicinity of the Labadie Banks, so the seas tended to build up in a chaos of conflicting wave motion. Having been in a hurricane off Bermuda, I had seen seas as big but never as sudden, turbulent and close together, which is what made this storm a new experience for me.

The tops of these waves swept decks clean—sometimes clean of crew, who were left dangling in the ocean at the ends of safety harnesses. Some of these harnesses broke, showing up many design flaws. Being lost like this is a slow death and many a sad story emerged after this storm. In hindsight it is easy to be critical, but unless you've actually been dismasted, rudderless, thrice rolled in cold water, you just cannot know how you'll react.

Frank Ferris, the 61-year-old skipper of *Ariadne*, whom I met before the start, is a case in point. His boat was rolled and dismasted and they had lost a crewman while another had suffered a bad head injury, so they abandoned ship for the liferaft.

Two hours later, just before the liferaft capsized, they used flares to attract the attention of a coaster. They were too exhausted to right their inflatable but clung to the outside clipped on by their safety harness, as the coaster *Manna* came close to pick them up. Sea conditions were extremely difficult and on *Manna*'s first pass, Frank unclipped himself and grabbed for the ladder, but was washed off by the next wave, never to be seen again. On the second attempt two of the crew made it to the ladder while on the third attempt, the next man got himself up the ladder but had failed to unclip his harness and was pulled back into the sea for good. The remaining survivor did not have the strength to pull himself up on the ladder and was washed away too. It was feared that he was swept under the propellers. He was never seen again either.

And so the horror story continued, as each yacht crew fought their own battle and the race progressed.

It hardly bothered the bigger boats who had rounded the Fastnet rock before the full fury of the storm struck. Jim Kilroy's *Kialoa* was first around and made it back to Plymouth, setting a course record of three days, three hours and fifty-two minutes in the process, but it was another American, Ted Turner in *Tenacious,* who won overall on adjusted time. On arrival, a journalist questioned Turner, asking him what he thought of the Irish Sea and English weather.

'Yes, fine.' Pause. 'And you'd better like it too.' Pause. 'Otherwise you'd all be speaking Spanish,' he continued, remarking that it's no use crying over the dead. 'The King is dead: long live the King.' At one point he said: 'That ain't the ultimate storm.'

On *Rapparee,* still out in the middle of it all as the storm raged on, we were lost among the giant waves without purpose and direction. A near fatal wave struck on Tuesday morning and nearly rolled us right over; fortunately the righting moment stopped us doing a full 360-degree turn, but it did knock out the mast-head gear. One time our navigator took off from his bunk and rocketed right across the cabin, fracturing a window on the other side; it was a wonder he did not fracture his skull.

In the fullness of time, the storm blew itself out. We missed our radio, which might have told us how our companions were faring and generally kept us in touch with the outside world. This finally got in touch with us in the shape of a helicopter that we spotted hovering on the horizon, so we produced our emergency hand-held VHF radio, which had a limited radius. Eventually the chopper was raised on the emergency Channel 16 and we asked for a position check. The reply came back calmly enough:

'We read you clearly, Yacht *Rapparee,* but cannot come to your assistance at this moment. We are endeavouring to pick up some bodies from the water.' That was our first intimation of how seriously wrong the race could have gone.

At that time I had wanted to continue in the race; but in view of the likely anxiety ashore and the risks should it blow up again, the skipper did the right thing which was to make for the nearest port of Dunmore East, that hospitable safe haven, on the south-eastern tip of Ireland.

'Land ahoy!' our bank clerk shouted in excitement the following evening on sighting Hook Head. Our progress through the day had been monitored by another helicopter, a spotter plane and a passing Russian freighter, who kindly came to offer his help, but we could still manage on our own.

A crowd gathered to cheer us in. It transpired that *Rapparee* was one of the last yachts accounted for and that this had caused a great deal of worry. Our position report the previous day had not, we were told, been relayed correctly by the RAF helicopter—which is unusual; undoubtedly this was on account of the pressures of the search and rescue operations. My own family had lost no sleep—I forgot to tell them I was crewing in this race. Ignorance is bliss!

The Royal Ocean Racing Club, who organized the event, conducted an official enquiry into the race and, though it made fascinating reading, they did come out of it very well. Perhaps an impartial panel might have produced a more useful report.

There are several valuable lessons to be learned from that Fastnet: the principal one is that you should stay with your boat. This is your best liferaft. Seven lives were lost in incidents associated with emergency rafts, of which three were directly attributable to the failure of the raft. All of the yachts, which these seven people abandoned, were subsequently found afloat and towed to harbour. In short, it is asking a great deal of any very small craft to expect it to provide safe refuge in conditions which overwhelm a large yacht—but this is what liferafts are expected to do.

Another valuable lesson, which was hardly referred to in the official enquiry at all, is to keep all crew sealed below deck as much as is possible. Then, no matter what happens, the boat can roll around until the storm abates; it is your best chance of surviving in such conditions.

Dunmore East was a safe haven, but it was not Cowes, where the Fastnet Race finishing line was. I left knowing full well that I would have to complete that course at some stage in the future.

Meanwhile, though, there was a much greater challenge which remained incomplete, and that was the crossing of the Atlantic single-handed. Somehow I had to prove to myself and the world that I could take on the Atlantic and get to the other side.

14

Single-handed to the West Indies

LIKE A LITTLE child who falls into the mill-stream while catching minnows, I just couldn't wait to catch minnows—and fall into the mill-stream—again. September of that year found me at Penzance on the south-west tip of England, my new boat (*Kilcullen II* in spite of not being an inflatable) pointing out to sea. I was about to compete in the Mini-Transat single-handed race, 4,000 miles to Antigua, West Indies. The call of the Atlantic was too strong for me. *Kilcullen II* was a proper little yacht at 21 feet, with a lifting keel and of foam sandwich GRP construction. She lay snugly in Penzance Harbour while, together with 34 other single-handers, some in bare feet, we were guests in the Mayor's parlour for a pre-race reception. Ironically, several boats damaged in the Fastnet storm still lay in the harbour looking a sorry sight.

It had been a struggle to get this far. I had sold virtually everything I owned, had sailed her 2,000 miles to qualify, and now here I was in a mixed group of loners gathered to meet Penzance officials.

'We have a great reputation here for shipwrecks, you know,' the mayor said cheerfully, and talked of the plundering, scavenging and salvage of wrecks that went on until the good citizens whom he represented (God help them) mended their ways.

Single-handed sailors are, by nature, a very individualistic variety of people. Some are—perhaps in my case—schizophrenic in personality, one side being a social and party-loving gregarious type, the other being a complete introvert, with an isolationist's desire to be alone, cut off from fellow men.

There is some driving inner force, not necessarily going out of its way to court danger, but needing to meet a challenge and to stand out from the crowd.

Critics have labelled single-handed sailing as downright unsafe, unseamanlike and foolish. Perhaps. However, many innovations in sailboat design have come from this sort of sailing, and have added considerably to safety features. Contrary to what anyone may say, there is still a long way to go in the design of small, safe and seaworthy craft—boats that will stand up to the rigours of the ocean being the ultimate test. Granted, in ordinary circumstances, people should be strongly advised not to set out across the Atlantic in boats this size, but if a man or woman prove a craft's seagoing ability by safely crossing the Atlantic alone in the design, the lesson will not be lost on the family man or weekend sailor with young kids or an inexperienced crew.

Since the early days in the 1960s of single-handers like Bill King, Alec Rose and Francis Chichester, single-handed voyages have become so common that they are no longer novel. But it still remains one hell of an adventure to sail a small boat alone across the Atlantic ocean. And while many have more sense than I'll ever have, many more aspire to crossing the ocean alone. However, the make-up of that gathering of individuals in the Mayor's parlour will always be in a minority. Few arm-chair adventurers ever cast their mooring lines adrift; instead they live their adventures through the minority. There are many things I've always wanted to do, but it is unlikely that I ever will, except through books which have enabled me to live their adventures.

The establishment yachting press had been critical of the Mini-Transat. Indeed the French entrants incurred a peculiar risk of their own: the Race rules stated that all entries must be under 6.5 metres, but under French law it is illegal to go more than 100 kilometers from the French coast on a boat this size, so all French entrants were breaking the law and liable to prosecution on returning home.

Original entries were restricted to 50, of whom 48 qualified and now only 32 entrants finally mustered for the start at noon, Saturday 29 September. We were all nervous, the equinox gales and other filthy weather patterns of the previous few days had delayed entrants in arriving and the forecast was not good. The first leg of the course was to take us south across the Bay of Biscay to the Canary Islands for a stopover before heading straight for Antigua in the West Indies.

In order to catch the tide, the tiny fleet locked out from the dock nearly two hours before the start. It was quite a moving spectacle with wives, families, well-wishers and clicking cameramen recording it all on film. Some sculled, others rowed while many more were towed out since none of the boats had engines. I was lucky in that Mother, Aunt Sheila and two sisters Annmarie and Frances along with a good friend Kevin O'Farrell, had made the difficult journey from Ireland to see the *Kilcullen* off.

Single-hander Amy Boyer cried for a bit.   A young girl with buckets of gumption and personality, Amy had shipped her boat from California to race together with Norton Smith in another boat, built for the race and appropriately named *American Express*. At 34, Norton was one of the older race participants, and in preparation the previous week, he made sure to get to bed early, eat the right food and stay off the beer, so everybody reckoned that he was an obvious candidate to die from excess health.

It was the day the Pope landed in Ireland and in salute I flew the papal flag. Manoeuvring in the headwind became tricky as the big moment approached and the race started. Soon the fleet, racing straight south clear of land, spread out considerably. I'll never forget the sudden isolation after all the excitement of the start. It was in effect going from one extreme to the other. Being alone does strange things to the mind, and there is always a danger that it will drive you to a mental asylum, as happened to one participant to my knowledge.

The closest boat to the *Kilcullen* for a short while was *Julienas,* surfing along happily in the large waves, skippered by Frenchman, Philipe Harele, at 48 by far the oldest man in the race. He had also designed his own boat together with many of the other entries. *Julienas* was named after the French town noted for fine wines, and he called all of his boats after different wines.

Norton Smith took an early lead. The boat had many fine design features, not least being water ballast tanks built into either side of the hull. 'It was like having four gorillas sitting on the weather rail,' was how Norton described the 600-pound ballast tanks on *American Express,* the reason that he had now taken this early lead on the wind. Personal comfort is critical, according to Norton, in the quest to win on yacht races. 'This is not so that I can take it easy, but in order that I can get the most from myself when the going gets rough.' He was obsessed with a good diet and even had green vegetables growing on board according to one source. I suspect this, though I do know he had fresh potatoes while the best I could ever rise to was 'Supermash'.

Another yacht, racing along well was *Petit Dauphin 11* skippered by Daniel Gilard, winner of the first Mini-Transat run two years previously. His boat was a new prototype designed for the race and at 3,085 pounds was one of the heaviest entries, complementing Daniel's pot belly, while Norton's *American Express* weighed only about 1,985 pounds

Dropping behind, Bob Salmon the organizer, in *Anderson Explorer,* was also racing while his good wife Beryl looked after the administration ashore. A man in the old British school, but most certainly not an establishment figure, Bob was a great participant but not motivated towards winning. He was much too civilized for the hard cut and thrust of keen competition. The race was his original idea and came one time after he had landed in Antigua in the West Indies following a yacht delivery trip.

'My!' says he, ' wouldn't this be a glorious spot to finish a transatlantic race.' And so it happened.

By darkness everybody had disappeared, but the wind persisted as strong as ever, powering the *Kilcullen* through each wave. Happily the self-steering system, christened Molly Malone, worked fine and it was possible to prepare an evening meal and sort out the mess below after the turmoil of the start. The system took on a personality all of its own, and in time I started to talk with Molly; it was like having another hand on board. Made by a French company, it is a very clever device which takes the energy from the water when you go off course to bring you back on line.

That evening I wrote in the log: 'This is a daft competitive sport, here I am, all alone, racing against competitors I cannot see. The real competition will be with myself and the elements.'

However we were still within VHF radio range, a mandatory piece of equipment for all the entrants, and it was Amy Boyer who first broke the silence. Her boat, *Little Rascal,* was named after a nickname she had earned at high school.

'This is *Little Rascal* calling, *Little Rascal, Little Rascal,* can anybody out there hear me...'Amy bellowed out in her sharp Californian accent. A pretty, hard-nailed and very determined young lady, she had had to get a letter from her mother giving her permission to compete in the race since she was under 21.

'Hello Amy, come in, this is Norton, do you read me? Over,' her fellow Californian spoke before I and, it later transpired, all other shipping in the area, had the chance to answer her call.

'What speed are you doing Amy?'

'Five knots. What's yours?' she replied.

'Seven knots.'

'You BUM!' Amy said with emotion as her words vibrated through the tiny VHF and the conversation concluded; however, later Norton gave her some advice when her self-steering broke down.

On board the *Kilcullen* we were doing six knots at the most so, at this rate, Norton would have a clear lead within a few days.

It was not long, though, before much of the fleet was out of VHF range and most had difficulty picking up anybody, with Amy being the one exception. In her forthright approach, the girl had some amazing link-ups.

My guess is that there are few radio officers at sea who would not answer this sort of call:

'This is *Little Rascal* ... I am a lone American girl sailing across the Atlantic in a 21-foot boat; if anybody can hear would they please answer?'

One time her sextant and navigation was way off and a ship's officer spent close to half an hour explaining to her how to adjust the sextant. Another story she related herself:

'I got hold of this English radio operator and he tried to pick up on me. It was really sick. I was sitting here asking his position and it turns out he was way north of me heading north. He was saying: "Do you have any men on your boat?" and "Do you want to come to my boat to make love, I'll meet you tonight." I couldn't believe the guy, he was just nuts. I couldn't get on the radio for hours on end because every time I got on, he was there.'

The going was very tough but, after a period of being seasick, I settled down to a routine. There were several gales and near gales that ravaged through the fleet and crossing the Bay of Biscay was turbulent. A week later, approaching the Finisterre area and the Spanish coastline, the fleet converged to negotiate

Cape Villano and infamous Cape Finisterre, which became the Cape Horn of the race, while some skippers stayed well out to sea. Meanwhile further west out on the Atlantic an intense low-pressure system was gaining momentum and moving east; the worst was yet to come.

The week that followed was a nightmare. Rather than staying inshore down along the coast of Portugal and Spain it would have been much wiser to stay well out to sea to go around it, though it meant sailing a longer distance.

In the storm and storms that followed there was little alternative but to ride them out under bare poles, taking all that the enormous waves could throw at the *Kilcullen*. Again there was no accurate way of measuring the size of the waves and the strength of the winds save to say that no less than four competitors were knocked out of the race through gear failure, boats starting to break up and sheer exhaustion. It was fortunate that no lives were lost.

I was worried sick about everything. The rudder bolts working loose, the leaking keel, the mast, a tear in the sails, my own physical and mental shape and so on. The tension, nervousness and frustrations of getting this far were starting to penetrate. There was no way I could allow myself to fail now; I had to succeed; there must be no turning back.

Being in the shipping lanes was also a nightmare. I felt helpless bobbing around in the storms with little likelihood of being seen and every chance of being run down. The lightning and thunderstorms experienced close to land were the worst, followed by the cold rain which fell in buckets.

The one consolation was that other competitors must be experiencing the same conditions.

'It's a race, it's a race, it's a race . . .' I kept telling myself. 'Forget the survival tactics, you can't be conservative for ever, the wind has moderated, you must get sail up, you must get going . . .' And go I did, but first it was necessary to climb the mast and replace a halyard which had come adrift, a difficult business even at the best of times and not made easier by a turbulent sea. Indeed it was a last-minute addition to my gear in Penzance that made this possible. It was a special lightweight galvanized folding wire ladder, standard issue to Royal Society for Prevention of Cruelty to Animals inspectors; it was kindly donated by Brian Sanders from his RSPCA kit.

It was marvellous to be under way again. The wind went around to the west and the seas eased. Soon I felt that we would be in the influence of the long overdue Azores High and warmer southern weather. Later I learned that the storms we had come through were some of the worst on record in this area for this time of the year.

'You're lucky to be in one piece,' Mark Arnold, third officer on a British merchant ship the *Eloiseid* informed me. We had made contact on the VHF radio and he kindly gave a position report adding: 'There is a Low way off in the North Atlantic, but there is not really much happening or anything for you to worry about.' He did express surprise on learning the size of *Kilcullen*: 'I reckoned our ship was small, but yours, phew! ... Rather you than me, good luck, mate!'

Now fifteen days out of Penzance, the effect of the isolation was beginning to take hold. The nights were the worst and I feared the awful nightmares in addition to the worry that I would not wake to the alarm, set to go off every hour to check for shipping. I kept telling myself that this was nothing by comparison to the inflatable boat crossing; perhaps, but how in heaven's name did I survive that, I wondered.

'Oh Molly where would we be without you?' I wrote about the self-steering system in the log. Sometimes I imagined Molly to be a great big stroppy woman with an enormous bust, hanging over the tiller, as she sat steering the *Kilcullen* through the swells. One time I heard voices on the deck which turned out to be the squeaks from the self-steering lines. Molly never talked much, but I constantly remember her singing songs such as 'The Rose of Tralee', 'Galway Bay' and of course her own song with cockles and mussels, alive, alive o. . . . .

As the days passed, the *Kilcullen* edged further south and October 15th arrived, a day to celebrate my 24th birthday, alone. Lisbon now lay some 100 miles on the port beam and the great towering volcanic island of Tenerife some 700 miles to the south and west, while the wind started to swing around to the north. Perfect. The ship's log of that evening, as I celebrated with a bottle of beer, was full of self-analysis: 'If the truth be known, I'm happy; but oh! I'm getting old.'

For the first time it was possible to strip off the layers of clothes and set the spinnaker. With a tail wind, now piping up to force four, everything was perfect and within four days at the most I expected to make Tenerife.

At night time I played it safe and dropped the spinnaker in favour of two large headsails winged either side of the mast and supported by poles while the mainsail was dropped. This was a tragic mistake. Around 0100 hrs, as I lay in my bunk, the movement of the boat changed as the wind increased. 'There is nothing to be concerned about,' I thought to myself; 'sure, what can go wrong with no main or spinnaker set and only two foresails? Besides, we're clear of the shipping lanes.' The bunk was also cosy and inviting as I remained there curled-up and half-asleep, dreaming.

Then a sudden gust of wind came out of nowhere and practically lifted the *Kilcullen* out of the ocean. The clouds blotted out what little moon there was and put out the last of the stars, which had been shining brightly just half an hour previously. Now it was total darkness, the sea impossible to distinguish from the sky. One just listened to it. We raced along the wavetops while Molly Malone worked hard to hold the *Kilcullen* stern to wind. The roar of the *Kilcullen* surfing downwind and the turbulence of the ocean drowned all other sounds. I didn't hear the mast breaking.

It was as if a bomb had exploded. Everything on deck was a shambles. What remained of the mast, fractured in three places, lay limp in the water as the *Kilcullen* rolled helplessly in the Atlantic swell.

My world was shattered. Having come so far and having been through so much, I could not accept that the impossible had happened. Another failure! A stump stood where the mast once was. I forced myself to sit down and think constructively; there was no alternative this far out in the ocean on my own.

Through the night I salvaged what I could and fell down into the bunk, exhausted.

Dawn brought revived spirits, but the nightmare was now very real. With the wind now settled in the north and dropping, I could not make for Portugal. Would it be possible to make up a jury rig and get myself to Tenerife? At all costs I determined to stay in the race. Even if it took another year, I would make it across the Atlantic this time somehow.

It was a simple miscalculation that broke the mast; ironically I had been too conservative. With the two spinnaker poles attached to one spot on the mast, and no mainsail to compensate the thrust, the mast was wrongly loaded when a foresail backed, and gave under the strain.

O'Coineen was not finished yet. 'Fight, fight,' I kept telling myself and that is exactly what I did. Fortunately the wind virtually disappeared, and a full and difficult day was spent concocting a jury rig by lashing two spinnaker poles together and erecting them beside the stump. Once at Tenerife I could see to getting a replacement mast—somehow.

As luck would have it, the following day the wind filled in from the north and, by all sorts of imaginative means, a good spread of canvas was hung, driving the *Kilcullen* along at an amazing three and a half knots towards Tenerife. There was still hope. If only the wind would hold, there would be a good chance of making Tenerife before the start of the second leg.

I determined to stop a ship as we got back closer to the shipping lanes and, on the second attempt, a coastal steamer altered course on seeing the flares. Unfortunately, the emergency VHF antenna, designed for such emergencies as this, was useless with flat batteries so it would be necessary to go alongside a ship to get a message home. Firstly I wanted to report my position, to say that everything was O.K. and that the *Kilcullen* did not require rescue, and secondly to request that the boat builder give me credit and fly me a mast to Tenerife. Unfortunately, on discovering that I did not require rescue—and hence salvage for them—they cleared off.

Then, just before sunset of the following day, 19 October, a tiny speck—slowly growing bigger—loomed over the horizon. It was not unlike Hallowe'en as I lit the sky with my few remaining parachute flares. The ship stopped. Called the *Auto Sceptre*, she was a gigantic orange-painted tanker, registered in Liverpool.

Her crew lined the decks. It took a full thirty minutes to slow down enough for me to go alongside as she circled. I needed to go alongside to ensure that my message, written for home on a piece of paper, was not garbled.

A crewman threw a light line which was then tied to a heavier one which I rapidly secured to the *Kilcullen*'s bow. However, by the time this was done, we had been drawn back under the tanker's enormous stern and, while the great propellers were stopped, the ship still had way on. Had the *Kilcullen* still had a mast up to this point, she would not have had one any longer!

As each ocean swell rolled, the *Kilcullen* was being squeezed up under the curved stern; in a matter of seconds I was fighting for my boat, trying to hold her off with my back up against the rusty sides. Nobody on the side of the ship could even see the *Kilcullen* now and, above the noise from the low revving motors, they could not hear my shouting and near-panic screams.

It was a dilemma whether to stay in my position to stop the *Kilcullen* from going under the stern, or to race forward to cut clear of the bow line which was dragging the *Kilcullen* forward and under. There seemed to be no way out. The smart thing might have been to jump clear and save my own life, leaving the *Kilcullen* to be mashed up under the tanker's stern. But I couldn't yet bring myself to abandon ship, hoping as I was that the ship's crew would leave go the bow line.

'Use your rudder, use your rudder!' Magic words from a sharp crewman who managed to get a view of my dilemma through a hawser hole high up on the tanker's stern.

The advice worked. As if by a miracle, the *Kilcullen* coasted clear: with the continuous forward movement the rudder proved effective. I was so intent on fighting to stop going under that this simple and obvious solution had never crossed my mind.

Once again in control, I passed my message to the tanker to relay home, which they kindly did, while all offers of help and provisions were turned down since outside assistance would automatically disqualify me from the race.

The sun set gloriously that evening as the tanker disappeared slowly over the horizon. The *Kilcullen* was a mess from the dirty tanker ropes, bent and broken guard-rails and stanchions—all covered in an orangey-brown rust chips from the tanker's side. The hull was also badly scraped but, happily, remained structurally sound.

Five days later, in the early hours of the morning (but not before the *Kilcullen* had almost been run down again at night), the lighthouse on the northern tip of Tenerife loomed dead ahead. It was one of the most beautiful sights I ever saw. However, getting across the finishing line at the port of Darsena Pesquera, a small commercial harbour about three miles north of Santa

Cruz, the capital, was easier said than done. To get assistance now would mean failure, but with the jury rig I could not sail to windward and remained at the mercy of the cross-current.

I succeeded by virtually rock-hopping along the coast, slowly inching my way towards the finish line. It was nerve-racking and the whole exercise took about six hours—but I remember grasping the finishing post, I remember my hands on the hot melting tar on the wooden stake, so get there I finally did!

One hour later two other contestants, with masts, crossed within minutes of each other. I was not last and, once in harbour, was given a festive welcome by Amy and Bob together with all the other competitors. That evening as we compared notes, there were many stories to tell.

15

Arrested

THE EUPHORIA on arrival in Santa Cruz was short-lived. Bob Salmon verified my arrival time on the log while Beryl Salmon laced my coffee with whiskey to celebrate. The first thing, though, was to call home, which was possible on Bob's VHF on a local radio station link-up.

Since the mast was such a specialized bit of marine equipment there was no suitable mast available locally. Anything which was not purpose-built for the *Kilcullen*'s particular rig would be likely to let me down on the Atlantic crossing. Only three days remained to the start of the next leg: only three days to obtain and install a proper new mast. The tanker had been as good as its word and conveyed my message home, so Arthur Edmonds, the builder, already had a new mast waiting to forward from Heathrow: all he needed was my arrival at Santa Cruz—and money. He took the *Kilcullen*'s trailer at home in place of cash payment for the mast, but getting the mast, all thirty feet of it, to the island on time would be another problem. It would take a miracle to get it here to the island in time for the start, I was told, since it had to go via Madrid and possibly Las Palmas and would take at least two weeks. Wherever I turned I was told: 'Mañana—tomorrow!' I suppose as an Irishman I could scarcely protest, reminded as I was of Brendan Behan's quip when asked: 'What word have you got in your country that expresses the same as the Spanish word Mañana?' 'We have no word that conveys the same sense of urgency,' Behan replied.

My sense of urgency was acute to the point of desperation, but I kept running into blank walls until, at a reception in the plush Club Rio Nautico de Tenerife, I heard that the Vice-President of Iberia, the Spanish National Airline, was present. Swiftly I got an introduction, though I looked like a tinker, and I persuaded him to use his influence to speed the mast from Heathrow to Tenerife.

'This is like the Olympics,' I explained. 'Ireland's national honour is at stake. Everybody follows this race. Spain must help!' I pleaded, fully aware that few at home could care less.

'It is hard, Señor, to find ten metres free in a 'plane for a mast so long,' the Vice-President explained, but he kindly agreed to do what he could.

That was Thursday evening and the following morning I was on the telephone to my influential new friend. He could, it seemed, work miracles: on Saturday morning, as most of the competitors still in the race made for the starting line—over a third of the fleet was already knocked out—word came through that the mast had arrived at Santa Cruz airport. Only fifteen miles now between my mast and my boat—but could I get a van or trailer?

The heat, now approaching mid-day, was oppressive. On the main road I spotted a small truck that would do the job nicely and I flagged it down. The unfortunate driver did not know what hit him. As I had hardly slept in the last 48 hours and my clothes needed washing and I needed a shave, I looked a real tramp. I had sent a bundle of all my clothes off to the laundry but had not had a chance to pick them up. But the truck, carting vegetables, was ready enough to abandon its round when I waved a bundle of pesetas in the driver's face.

So off we raced—or clattered—to the airport in the antique ventilated truck. 'Muchas gracias, muchas gracias!' I kept saying to the driver, urging him on across the mountain to the airport. This was my first time actually seeing the island, since arrival three days previously. I had been so busy dashing around, organizing provisions and repairs and obtaining the new mast that I had had no chance to notice the beauty of the place, until that point. It was such a shame, to struggle for a month across the stormy sea to get here and now to be struggling equally to get away.

Of course I had forgotten about Customs. I raced straight through the airport and, as it transpired, the high-security area.

I also carried a camera to document the event. Without going through any of the normal procedures I located the mast—a long object protruding, with 'O'Coineen' written all over it. Fortunately I had my passport along for identification and naively thought that we could simply walk away with the mast.

'No señor,' shouted the Customs official: while the cargo had enjoyed special treatment from the Airline, the Government Customs service would waive no rules. We were told that it would be Monday before clearance could be obtained and, besides, the mast was subject to a heavy import tax.

In desperation I trotted out the Olympics story again, making out how important the whole thing was, but the seed fell on stony ground, that is, till I met Jesus. Another miracle-worker As the chief airport Customs official—and an English-speaker to boot—with his help the forms got filled faster than pork pies on a production line. To lend further urgency to the task, I kept my cine camera whirring to record the event. 'This film is for Irish Television,' I explained. A pity the film had run out.

All clear now—except that first we had to get back to Santa Cruz to fill in more forms while Jesus telephoned ahead. By this time my vegetable truck driver was on edge and it was a job to persuade him to come back to the airport again. The business was getting a bit too much for him. 'Muchas gracias, muchas gracias!' I kept saying.

Back at the airport for the second time, during a break as the final forms were being completed, I disappeared with the camera to the runway, having bought another roll of film. My idea was to film a plane landing, as if the mast was in it, to capture the atmosphere of my emergency. Little did I realize that we were in a high-security area.

A cloaked figure approached from the left. I took little notice and went on filming as an enormous jet landed. It was exciting being so close to the flying monster. The cloaked figure continued his approach, he wore a funny looking hat. Rather than doing the sensible thing and staying still I ran away from him. I had nothing to hide but, in the heat of the moment, I could not tolerate the thought of wasting more time explaining to the guard about the race, the mast, how we had to get to the start and so forth in broken English and Spanish.

I naively thought that as soon as I disappeared he would not

bother me. I'd never had the pleasure of meeting the Guardia
Civil up to that point.

Fortunately I spotted him going for his gun and, with the
corner of my eye, saw him aim it. Instantly his message, clearer
than words, struck home. No, he did not pull the trigger but I
stopped dead in my tracks and instantly dropped everything
putting my hands in the air—just as you see on television or the
movies.

The Guardia Civil had a fierce look about him. Now I learned
why these are the dreaded strong men of Spain with the authority
to shoot on sight. On top of that, if so inclined, they can slap
you in jail for up to 72 hours, incommunicado. He caught me
roughly by the arm, frisked his subject, and dragged him to a
small room with solid iron bars on the window at the corner
of the large airport freight building. Here more of his friends
were waiting to question me. It was only later I realized that
they had been watching my movements at the airport, unaware
of the mast problem. They suspected me of being possibly a spy,
taking photographs in a high-security area, or possibly a terrorist
about to highjack a 'plane.

Apparently the vegetable truck driver had seen the arrest from
a distance and decided, while the going was good, to get the
hell out of the place, not wishing to tangle with the dreaded
Guardia Civil. Unfortunately I had handed over most of my
remaining money to him at that stage.

'Irelande, Irelande,' I kept saying and tried to tell them about
the race. The word Ireland, though, instead of generating
goodwill as it normally does when you travel, compounded the
situation since they associated it with the IRA.

I had really landed myself in it this time. Hopes of making
the start of the race in time began to disappear and they left me
over an hour in the small stuffy room before a good English-
speaking guard was found. By that time, all sorts of possibilities
were going through my mind; would they slap me in jail, would
I have to await trial, where would it all end?

It took some time to explain my story and, eventually, on
contacting Jesus in the Customs area, they started to believe the
story, but not enough to let me go. Fortunately I still had the
number of the Irish Consul, a Spaniard, the man through whom
I had obtained money. He agreed to come to the airport and

vouch for me. It was a relief to be free again, though by that stage several hours had passed. Eventually we found a truck but, by the time we made it back to the harbour, the race had started and it was getting dark.

Through the night we worked, until about four a.m. when I collapsed in the bunk with exhaustion. It had been a nightmare getting the mast up in the dark, but everybody was very helpful and appreciated the urgency and determination. I considered leaving there and then, and catching up on sleep while at sea with the auto pilot connected up. Luckily a helper persuaded me not to.

It was in fact 1600 hours the following afternoon before the *Kilcullen* eventually got under way, a full 24 hours after the other competitors, which was a lot of ground to make up. But the boat's strong point was downwind sailing, as this leg would be in the trade winds, so there was still a good chance of catching up. Unfortunately the laundry, where all of my clothes were, save the dirty trousers and T-shirt I had on, was closed for it was now Sunday. Notwithstanding the prospect of being naked for days on end, in the lush warm trade winds it would not bother me at all.

The relief at getting to sea again was enormous. After the four frantic days ashore, I longed to be alone. Alone with my thoughts, and with 2,700 miles of open ocean ahead.

As I was swept south and west away from the Canary Islands, I was very nervous and lacked confidence in the new mast and rig. Ironically a local yacht club race that first day, in much larger yachts, was called off because the winds were too strong. The main Mini-Transat fleet the previous day had had a spectacular start, with Norton Smith once again taking an early lead. He was untouchable, an excellent sailor with a fast boat.

Amy Boyer was not so lucky, having been placed 11th in the first leg. She had been the first woman home, despite a cracked mast which was repaired in Tenerife. Twenty hours out of Tenerife, *Little Rascal* was thundering westwards: 'I was hoisting the spinnaker when the boat broached. There was a big thud. All I saw was a huge tail in the water then there was nothing,' Amy said afterwards.

Whatever owned that huge tail managed to loosen *Little Rascal*'s keel. Amy returned to harbour depressed, but after five days and repairs, set out bravely again to make a very quick crossing and win the ladies' prize by a mere five hours ahead of Brigitte Aubry.

Not far ahead of the *Kilcullen* 48-year-old Philippe Harle, who had finished fourth in the first leg, was having the greatest adventure and race of his life boat for boat with Daniel Gilard, who had been placed third. For three days they raced within sight of each other and, at times neck and neck, battling it out for lead positions.

There were several other personal races within races going on while during the first week I rested a great deal after the ordeal ashore, leaving Molly Malone to do a lot of the work while I carried a conservative spread of canvas. By this time the beautiful north-easterly trade winds had settled in and at one stage we ran for four solid days before dropping the spinnaker. Of course the halyard positions would constantly have to be adjusted, with chafe being a constant worry.

Every so often we would get a tropical squall line coming through but normally we could see it well in advance in the beautiful clear sky and shorten sail. However, on getting closer to Antigua some weeks later the weather once again became unsettled.

A French competitor on board *Tiki,* some 900 miles out, was not so lucky when a massive line-squall came through before he had the opportunity to shorten sail so he tried to ride it out: 'I couldn't leave the helm for fear that she'd be broached and rolled over with me up on deck,' the Frenchman reported, so he hung on.

'The speed was fantastic. The whole boat vibrated madly as she took off and tore through the spuming wave crests. Then there was nothing. Silence, it was all over.' His mast was broken in several places. Nonetheless, as I had in the first leg, he rigged a jury mast and managed to finish the race without assistance. And though he would probably have been able to raise a jury rig anyhow, the time he had spent learning how I had coped north of Tenerife in similiar circumstances had helped him considerably.

Happily, on board the *Kilcullen,* the entire 2,700 miles passed virtually without incident as I gradually caught up with the main fleet. I remained very conservative and stayed out of the sun as much as possible. The water supply became contaminated with some bugs from the Canaries; fortunately there was plenty of canned foods with liquids.

The fear of landfall kept creeping up. Antigua, being a low-lying island, would be easy to miss and I found it a bit worrying not having had any navigation check, just relying on my celestial calculations and a mass of figures. To run into trouble at this stage would be disastrous, as happened to Eric Legendre in *Sainte Sophie*.

He was within an hour of six other competitors, the main pack. Lack of sleep waiting for a landfall had lulled him into believing unquestioningly in his plotted positions. He failed to check his charts and, as a result, piled up on a reef at the north end of the island, fourteen miles from the finishing line. He was out of the race.

There are few pleasures in life better than making a landfall with precision after nearly three weeks at sea. Without fuss the *Kilcullen* crept across the line and into English Harbour early in the morning while everybody slept.

For me it was a magic moment. I was glad to slip in without a great parade. The *Kilcullen* was a credible sixth on time over the second leg and eighteenth overall, despite all the mishaps, out of 25 entrants who eventually made it to Antigua. Norton Smith went home to California with his first prize, and Jean Luc van den Heede, an enormous bearded French schoolteacher, took second place, followed by Daniel Gilard in third slot. The great friendship that existed between the competitors was memorable—in harbour even loners enjoy each others' company: Brigitte Aubry and Jacques de Ruck of Belgium enjoyed it so much that they were standing together before the altar a few short weeks later.

Originally it was my plan to return to my work in journalism in Dublin, but what was the point in selling the boat and returning in the middle of winter? The only person who would take pleasure in it would be the bank manager on getting his loan repaid. Instead I decided to continue on round the world in the *Kilcullen* after staying a few months in the West Indies.

Perhaps it's the West Indies that does things to people—I too fell in love. Initially I thought that she was a rich American chick while she thought that I was a rich Irish yacht owner. Once we discovered the truth about each other, we decided that—what the hell!—poverty is romantic. Her name was Suzanna.

16

Becoming a lord

SANTA MARIA la Redonda is a small island in the lesser Antilles, situated fifteen miles NNW of Montserrat and off the usual shipping lanes; Christopher Columbus found the place on his second voyage of discovery. It rises steeply 1,000 feet out of the sea and is impossible to land on because it has no beach and the sea constantly surges over its sheer rocks. So at least Columbus reported when he named the island on 11 November 1493. But Columbus obviously got it wrong, for in Antigua I was told of the lost Irish Kingdom on the Island. I consulted *Time-Life:* 'The island is chiefly interesting for its total insignificance,' it said. 'The two major events in its history occurred in the late nineteenth century when natives from Montserrat began phosphate digging and an obscure Irishman landed and proclaimed himself king...' I decided I had to go and take a look for myself.

Curiously, the monarchy obtained the blessing of the Church and the consecration ceremony was correctly conducted with great pomp and all the rites of the Church. After many years of petitioning, the British Colonial Office recognized the Irishman's right to call himself King, though it did not completely recognize his right to ownership of the island, which is still in dispute between the Antigua and Montserrat governments.

From the establishment of the colonial powers, Spain, England, France and the Netherlands, to the coronation in 1880 of the first King, Philipe I or M.P. Shiel, a great author and science-fiction writer, the island was rarely visited by man. By the turn of the century, however, well over a hundred men lived on Redonda and worked the plentiful phosphate deposits. Today

9. Marblehead, Mass. Father Powell blesses *Kilcullen (I)* before sailing.

10. Halifax. Preparing for departure.

11. Halifax. All sail set, making for the open sea.

12. *Kilcullen (I)*. Repairs in mid-ocean.

13. *Kilcullen (II)* during sailing trials off Cork.

14. *Kilcullen (II)*. When I had a mast I might need to climb it to clear seized lines. From the top I had a bird's-eye view of the boat.

15. Following the old tall-ship guidelines, to pick up the trade winds just sail south and turn right when the butter melts.

16. On the summit of Santa Maria la Redonda Suzanna reads a proclamation . . . to an attentive booby bird.

17. Tortola, West Indies. *Kilcullen (II)* and Suzanna one week before we sailed onto the reefs.

18. Suzanna complete with everything salvaged from the wreck, including an Instamatic camera with which these pictures were taken.

19. Bits of the *Kilcullen* gathered together at dawn, four and a half hours after running aground.

20. Bleak view of the seas which pounded the *Kilcullen* to pieces. A few relics are seen on the right.

21. *Kilcullen (III)*. Taking delivery in Holyhead. I recall how frail she looked.

22. *Kilcullen (III)* crossing the Atlantic.

23. A few dolphins for company.

24. Bookwork on board the *Kilcullen*.

the island is again uninhabited though the kingdom is very much alive.

Though normally at residence in his Court-in-Exile at Arundel, Sussex, back in England, as luck would have it, the present King, Juan II —also a literary man—was visiting Antigua to write his novel, *So Say Banana Bird*. Otherwise known as Jon Wynne-Tyson, born in 1924, the present King is a fascinating man; Suzanna and I became quite friendly with him.

Juan II gave his blessing for a centenary expedition to the island and asked us to report on the state of the landing jetty since Hurricane David.

He further expounded on the kingdom's curious history. Matthew Dowdy Shiel, a Montserrat ship owner, said to be descended from the ancient High Kings of Ireland had (according to his son) 'the Irish foible of thinking highly of people descended from Kings . . .' Though difficult to prove or disprove, his claim from Ireland of the nineteenth century is not that inconceivable.

About the time of his son's birth he found himself sailing by Redonda. Surprisingly none of the colonial powers had yet claimed the island—it was not thought worth claiming, if the truth be known. So, delighted was he by the arrival of a man-child after nine daughters, that he decided to mark the occasion by annexing the island as a kingdom for the boy. If the merchant could not make his only son a king at home in Ireland, he would damn well make him a king somewhere else. And so it came to pass.

Curiously, the island of Montserrat where Shiel's family grew up was then an almost exclusively Irish domain, peopled by many of Oliver Cromwell's captives and other exiles from various turbulent stages of Irish history. Even to the present day, though links with Ireland have been lost by the passage of time and sheer distance, this beautiful Caribbean island, which the black natives call their 'Emerald Isle', is renowned for its Irish hospitality and the brogue of the natives.

Now, we're told, the right of kings devolves from God. So old man Shiel was adamant that his son would be crowned with all due observances on the island that he claimed. To officiate at the coronation he recruited his old and convivial friend, the Bishop of Antigua.

By all accounts the crowning on 21 July, 1880 was a gala

affair. Many ships gathered at anchor in the lee of the island. Father and son scrambled ashore along with the Bishop and sundry courtiers; they then made the arduous climb to the summit and there underwent the solemn ritual of anointment. And so, M.P. Shiel became King Philipe I of Santa Maria la Redonda. He also became a renowned short-story writer, poet, prophet and a philosopher, author of over 300 books now, alas, all unread.

Having learned this much of the Redonda story, back in Antigua with my new found companion, Suzanna, we hoisted the *Kilcullen*'s sail and left English Harbour, making for the lost kingdom with an air of eager anticipation.

Slipping out round the harbour entrance reef and into the fresh trade wind and long Atlantic rollers, we hoisted our large green, white and orange spinnaker; the *Kilcullen*, living up to her name from the pre-Christian hero of Ireland, surfed and rolled downwind like a skier; the tropical sun glinted in flashes off the wave tops and before long the kingdom of Santa Maria la Redonda appeared as a speck on the horizon.

As we drew closer and observed the rock rising sharply out of the blue sea, Redonda had a barren, eerie look about her— lonely, desolate, precipitous and forbidding. It was difficult to accept that at one time 130 people lived on this rock, rising sheer from the waves—it looked impossible to climb without a ladder.

In the twilight the towering cliff-face filled the sky and seemed to dwarf our tiny boat. Even with two anchors out it was difficult to sleep; the surf boomed, the seabirds screeched, and the moaning of the wind as it tore through the cliff-tops was nerve-racking. There was a large swell running, which broke on the rocks with a loud thundering roar, sending spray and white spume in all directions as each successive wave broke. Not long after, the round red sun sank down into the western horizon and the full moon rose to the east above the island, illuminating the cliffs.

The atmosphere was charged and magical as Suzanna and I waited for dawn, together with our new deck-hand, Peter Dix. A long lean figure, Peter wore round gold-rimmed glasses and bore a striking resemblance to James Joyce—or so I imagined. He had just flown in to Antigua from New York, then in the thick of winter, and was determined not to get a sun-tan while ostensibly writing an article for Runner Magazine on jogging holidays in the Caribbean. I believe he qualified for this assignment by having sailed in the Olympics and being well able to talk.

Peter claimed to know little about jogging; likewise, even at the best of times, this was one of the most unsuitable climates in the world for jogging. So what even if thousands of jogging fanatics are misled! At one stage he had Suzanna out jogging to make a nice photograph to complement the article. Through the night details of the JAs association came to light, namely 'Joggers Anonymous'—every time you gets the urge to go running you dial this special number and a man promptly calls around with a bottle of whiskey and a packet of fags to put your mind at ease.

At dawn, we breakfasted to the sound of screeching seagulls and prepared for our invasion. I sealed survival rations, provisions and a camera into watertight bags and tied them into our tiny inflatable dinghy, blown up for the occasion. Peter stayed to mind the ship while Suzanna and I headed ashore.

As we drew closer, the swell looked positively dangerous and worse than it seemed from a distance. By then it was too late to turn back and we got caught in the surge. Successive hurricanes and erosion over the decades had wiped out the old landing jetty – how on earth had they ever built it?—and what little foreshore there was was almost completely eroded. Now all that remained to greet us were giant boulders and dangerous rocks below sheer cliffs. It is not surprising that all the guide books say: 'Stay away, it's dangerous.'

Within seconds we were out of control, caught in an explosion of spray. I heard Suzanna scream. A breaking wave swept us out of the dinghy and into the hissing white surf. It was useless to fight it. Rocks would have floated in the surf. I could still hear Suzanna but could not see her; the dinghy had been washed away upside down like a matchstick. I felt myself being pushed along the rocks, then the water dropped away as quickly as it had come, and I scrambled up the slippery rocks, clear of the water, before another wave as big approached.

Suzanna could not be seen. As the undertow started she found herself jammed between two boulders—she could not get out! She thought that her hip was broken (it turned out just to have been badly bruised) and the succeeding waves were running clean over her so that she was being drowned. In true hero style, I raced back into the surf and somehow managed to haul her ashore.

Meanwhile Peter, feeling helpless on board the *Kilcullen,* jumped over the side and swam in to join us, being treated just as roughly by the sea in his turn though he landed at a safer spot.

We compared bruises and cuts; fortunately no serious injuries had been suffered and the dinghy had landed high and dry upside down with the gear still lashed in. Getting ashore had been a stiff challenge; getting back out would be the next problem, but we put it at the back of our minds and set out to exploring the island.

We set about occupying the Redondan General Post Office where we based ourselves as the invading army. First we had to break in by unscrewing the door lock. The wooden cabin contained a roof, four walls, a desk, two chairs and two mattresses, along with some other odds and ends such as an empty whiskey bottle and a cigarette box. Old magazines, including the *Economist, Time* and the *Financial Times* were scattered around the desk drawers. A selection of Redonda stamps, along with a tiny map of the island, were glued to the bare wall behind.

The island had a curious feeling surrounded in legend and mystery. It was hard to imagine King Felipe I here in the last century. We could even now look across the white-capped sea to the island of Montserrat in the distance, which he had described as being 'like the burial-place of Moses, wrapped in mystery'.

It was another day before, leaving Peter at base camp to watch the boat, we climbed to the plateau, where the miners lived, and scaled the summit. The miners had had an aerial tramway of which nearly all trace had now gone, thanks to rock falls, erosion and successive hurricanes. For us it was a difficult and dangerous climb, 500 feet up the gully, where the tramway eighty years previously had made an almost vertical climb.

Fritz Fenger, who cruised through the island on a 16ft batwing canoe before World War I, gave a fascinating report as to how he landed at a large buoy on Redonda's western shore. From here they lifted him, and his canoe, out of the water and onto a cable car which carried them both to the Manager's house 1,000 feet above.

'Two stout, heavy wire cables were stretched up the gorge

and firmly anchored at both ends. Upon each cable ran a trolly, from which was suspended a large iron bucket. When passengers or freight were to be raised the bucket at the top of the cliff was filled with water from a tank, and the lighter load at the bottom was quickly 'drawn up'.

As the day advanced and we kept climbing the sun grew very hot and pierced down from above, raising the temperature to about 110 degrees in the gorge. Occasionally our climbing caused minor landslides and small lizards would dart in all directions. We encountered some of the cactus plants, with heads like gnomes, that we had been warned about.

By noon time the gorge assumed all of the characteristics of an oven, and, without the hint of a breeze (being the sheltered side), the rocks had become too hot to touch. It was filled with volcanic gravel and had few resting places, so, having come this far, there was no alternative but to keep going.

Finally we made it to the plateau and in all directions we had a breath-taking view of the northern Caribbean. We enjoyed a tremendous feeling of freedom as we stripped off all our heavy clothes, worn for protection on the climb, and stood naked, cooled by the wind. The breeze rustled gently over the lush grass and dangerous cactus—otherwise there was the silence of nature and isolation in this uninhabited kingdom.

Below, the *Kilcullen*, between the rolling swell, looked tiny. Peter had very much regretted not being able to join us on the assault but it was reassuring to know he was keeping an eye on the boat.

We found the foundations of former buildings and the rusting machinery of the old phosphate mine. From the ridge a grassy slope descends at an angle of thirty degrees to the east and south. Broken water catchments and the foundation of the manager's house were on the slope to the north, which was capped with a pinnacle of large boulders.

Time was short, if we were to reach the summit, plant King Juan II's flag, the Irish tricolour, read out our proclamation, and avoid the risk of being stranded for the night.

As we made our way along the treacherous cliffs towards the summit, three quarters of a mile away, we considered what it must have been like for 130 men living together and working on this barren outcrop for months on end.

Fred W. Morse gives a vivid account of the primitive conditions the miners lived under, when he visited the island in 1890. He describes Sunday, their day off: 'After breakfast, the workmen were summoned by the bell to meet in front of the Master's House and answer to their names. In order to have better control over this men, Captain H—had devised the arrangement of dividing a man's weekly wages into seven portions instead of six, and obliging him to report at roll call on Sunday or forfeit one seventh of his weekly earnings. This method put them on their good behaviour during this day as well as others, whereas they had previously claimed Sunday as their own to do as they pleased. It was an interesting sight to see the line of black faces, varying in intelligence from refinement to brutishness. As the roll was called I was astonished to hear the names Michael and Patrick, coupled with Sweeney and Burke, names very familiar to my ears, but these responded to by men with shiny, ebony faces. On enquiry I learned that these men belonged in Montserrat, which was settled by Irish refugees whose family names had descended through their slaves to these miners.'

Both Suzanna and I were very worn out and, though we had food for munching, regretted our mistake in not bringing a water container. We were forced to stop and rest on many occasions, and I was thirsty enough to drink all of the Guinness brewery dry.

A drawback we encountered to exploring the island were the cactus which the workmen spoke of long ago as 'suckers'. They are, we are led to believe, almost unique to Redonda and dangerous. They resemble the prickly pear in form and have a yellow blossom. We kept well away and were as careful as could be under the circumstances with all of our movements. The joints of the cactus are thickly covered with thorns, from three quarters of an inch to an inch and a half in length and barbed at the tip. The joints are easily broken off and cling to anything upon which their spines can catch. When the barbed spine becomes embedded in the flesh it produces a poisonous sore unless removed at once; this is difficult and it is usually necessary to cut it out in order to remove it.

On reaching for a hand-hold I got a terrible shock. I had put it into a nest and, as I peered around the corner of the bush, a large Booby bird—a seabird about the size of a chicken—stood stock still and a bit startled. Bird and man stared at each other in silence. Undoubtedly the bird sitting on her eggs was surprised, but the thought of being frightened did not seem to cross the creature's mind—having had no previous contact with man. It had brown plumage, a blue/yellow beak and a white undercarriage, with duck-like feet that exposed this landed creature as a seabird. As we progressed we met hundreds of these pretty and friendly birds who nested all over the place, they were pleasant company, and did not squawk like seagulls. From time to time we met the Booby bird young who had not yet learned to fly; their plumage was a beautiful soft, virgin white.

We encountered no less than three false peaks—thinking each one was the summit—before finally reaching King Juan's Peak. The flag-pole still stood, but the King's Redonda flag, erected the previous April, had been blown away to shreds; there is little that can withstand the fury of a West Indian hurricane—the recent David being worse than most. The flag is a three-colour job running horizontally with blue on the bottom representing the sea, brown for the earth and green for foliage on top. Later we learned that the disintegrated April flag had been made by 'Queenie', the King's lovely wife Jennifer, in part out of an old pair of his pyjamas.

Then Suzanna produced one of the Redonda flags she had made while staying in English Harbour. We hoisted it with ceremony and read, to the whistling wind and a dazed Booby bird who stood on a nearby rock, our carefully worded proclamation.

It explained the nature of the *Kilcullen* Expedition; namely to commemorate Shiel the writer, re-establish the 'Irish connection' and to mark the centenary of the Realm. We were careful to emphasize that we recognized the Antigua Government to be legal owners of Redonda. Our interest was solely in promoting Juan II's literary and ecological kingdom.

Though some Antiguan officials do not believe him, Juan II, or Jon Wynne-Tyson, emphasizes that he has no political claims on Redonda and told us: 'My ruling ambitions for the island are cultural, not political. Antigua is understandably cautious about losing what may still be valuable phosphate deposits. However, from research carried out and people we talked to, mining on the island will never be a viable commercial propo-

136 The Unsinkable Kilcullen

sition for the future. The real bonus to Antigua lies in perpet-
uating rather than hindering the Shiel legend and making things
difficult for the King.'

The man who had succeeded the first King was the poet John
Gawsworth, who took the title Juan I. Sadly, as time progressed
Juan I developed a drink problem; the more he drank, the more
liberal he was in random bestowals of Redondan peerages. In
1954 he appointed a successor-King, Reg Hipwell, who died in
1964. By covenant this passed to Hipwell's son David, who died
in 1966, Juan I then sought capriciously and wrongfully to sell
his kingdom, and ran a want ad. in the *Times* to that effect.
Fortunately, he was prevented from committing this profane
crime in 1966 by certain officials of his court, called the 'Privy
Council of Five'. Meantime, Gawsworth drifted towards total
dissolution from drink and on his hospital deathbed in 1970, aged
58, in a state of enforced sobriety, passed over the title to the
publisher and writer Jon Wynne-Tyson.

Jon says that he became a reluctant monarch. He lacked kingly
ambition and, with little respect for royalty, was inclined to let
sleeping islands lie. Initially he kept quiet about his accession.
But as Gawsworth had made him his own and Shiel's literary
executor, he was enmeshed in the renewed interest in Shiel's life
and work. 'Redonda proves to us,' the King says, 'that all
monarchies, like all forms of power, are nonsense—but it is still
possible for that nonsense to be agreeable and lighthearted.'

As on the Plateau, the view in all directions from the summit
of Redonda was not one to be readily forgotten. To the north
lay St Kitts and Nevis in the sparkling Caribbean Sea. Montserrat
stood out to the south, while Antigua lay low to the east. Time
seemed to stay still and we stayed for longer than we should
have before sunset approached, mesmerized by it all.

Just enough time—and light—left to take some pictures.
Having left most of our clothes at the top of the gully, we had
only one pair of trousers between the two of us, so we wore
them in turns to make our pictures respectable. To give our
summit ceremony the respect it deserved, I had brought a tweed
cap and tie which flew in the wind.

Just behind King Juan's peak a lesser peak stood and, according
to our map, had no name; so we erected an Irish flag and decided
to call it Kilcullen's Mountain!

Then we scrambled down the mountain as the light faded. Back at the General Post Office we also hoisted the Redondan and Irish flags. Suzanna assumed the role of Postmistress, sealed a few hastily written letters and started to prepare for our treacherous return trip through the surf. I carefully taped our proclamation to the bare wall, screwed up the broken door and left the building as lonely and desolate as we had found it.

By now the short twilight of the tropics had been succeeded by darkness and the full moon loomed on the eastern sky. The breaking surf crashed on the shore with monotonous regularity. Thousands of miles from home, it was not difficult to believe that we sat on one of the most inaccessible islands in the world.

Though we approached the surf with some anxiety, getting off the island proved to be easier than coming in. I tied myself to the dinghy and the trick was to stand on a big rock, wait for a very big wave to come along and then throw myself into the water as it reached its highest level; the undertow will do the rest. (The sensation must be akin to being tipped into a hydro-electric fall pipe, but it turned out to be fairly safe.) Then swim away like a frightened rat to avoid being shattered on the rocks by the next wave.

The Redonda seabirds provided our alarm clock the following morning just before daybreak. Their cries and shrieks pierced the atmosphere from their hundreds of homes in the crevices and niches of the cliffs. The birds seemed to tell us that we were intruders, the island is better off without human kind which brings nothing but trouble wherever it goes.

Soon it was bright with the glorious Caribbean sunrise to the east, obscured by the cliffs, and time to go. It took a full hour to clear the anchors and free the lines which had chafed through a number of times during our two-day stay. With that, sails were hoisted and the *Kilcullen*'s long beat back to Antigua began.

Some time later, as a result of our exploits and having delighted the King, Suzanna was awarded the Juan Cross for valour and the title of Lady Suzanna of Potsdam, while I was appointed to the order of the Star of Redonda, Knight Commander. To be a Knight was a curious new experience. For good measure I became The Lord Kilcullen, so named after Kilcullen's mountain on the island.

By this time Peter Dix had gone back to New York and my

love affair with Suzanna blossomed.

Life took on a totally new dimension. Together we made plans to continue on around the world on board the *Kilcullen*.

First it would be a cruise north to Florida, some 1,000 miles. Then we would have to work for a while before trailing the *Kilcullen* across America to California. Since she was light and trailed easily, this American overland voyage promised to be an adventure in itself—going across the mountains the *Kilcullen* could double as a caravan.

From San Francisco I would sail her in the Transpac race to Hawaii, from there on to the Indian Ocean and on around the world home to Ireland, taking about three years. That, at any rate, was the plan!

Like all the Bahamas it is low-lying, with a maximum height of 160 feet over its fourteen miles, and is largely rock-bound. We came for two days but left after five—a hospitable island, San Salvador! The next leg up to Nassau, the capital of the Bahamas, some 150 miles away, promised to be tricky. From there it would be plain sailing across the Gulf Stream to Florida, some two hundred miles further on.

The day before the feast day of Saint Patrick, we negotiated the harbour exit, one which had been blasted out of solid rock. There was a fair swell running with a fifteen-knot stern wind. Suzanna was again very much on edge, as if she could smell something in the wind.

Under self-steering but with one of us on watch, our yacht merrily ran along her north easterly course before the long rolling Atlantic swell, unobstructed for thousands of miles. While the afternoon had been bright and sunny, it was dark and overcast by the time the black tropical night had fallen. Allowing for compass variation and tidal drift, I plotted our course to take us up the centre of the thirty-mile gap between the tip of Cat Island and the reefs off the end of Long Island, and up the centre of the Exuma Sound by dawn for a daytime arrival at Nassau.

Since we were not in any rush it seemed more prudent to run through the night under foresail alone, leaving the mainsail tucked around the main boom. With some fluky wind about, I resolved to keep a careful watch while old 'Molly Malone', our self-steering gear, took care to keep the *Kilcullen* on course.

Around midnight the wind increased as a frontal system started to come through, visibility decreased and the *Kilcullen* kept tramping along in fine fettle. It was pitch dark under a thick canopy of cloud, and near impossible to make out the bow from the cockpit. Still, our course allowed for plenty of leeway even in a three-knot cross-current. Moreover there was a reliable light marked on the relatively recent Admiralty Chart (1973) for the tip of Cat Island, so as a last resort we would have that light to guide us.

As the wind approached gale force, with big seas running, I dropped the foresail, leaving us to surf along at about three knots under bare poles.

Suzanna lay comfortably in her bunk. A sudden wave had thrown her onto the floor some half hour previously, but now she was well secured. Meanwhile I kept watch. I could have done with a little more visibility, but the compass was doing its job and I saw no need to worry.

Suddenly there was a terrifying crunch and the whole boat vibrated as the keel scraped the bottom. The movement on deck was violent, I raced forward to drop the anchor, which we always had 'on the ready' on the foredeck, and was nearly tossed overboard. Fortunately I grabbed a shroud and managed to crawl the rest of the way.

Out of the blackness from all sides came the roar, crash and gurgle of breaking surf. Masses of froth and spray swept across the *Kilcullen*'s decks. We were now at the mercy of the breaking seas tumbling headlong against the rugged deadly coral and volcanic rock.

The anchor was useless. Our emergency procedure of dropping anchor, lifting the keel and preparing to sail off was pointless. To combat that surf would have been like a grasshopper trying to fight a herd of stampeding elephants.

Suzanna was in a state of shock in the cabin, though she controlled herself remarkably well after being flung—yet again —out of her bunk, despite the leeboards. Searching frantically for her glasses or contact lenses she was near blind, though in the darkness they would hardly have made much of a difference.

I was faced with a difficult decision: Set some canvas and attempt to sail off, or go down below, seal the hatch, put up the stormboards and hope for the best. To try setting sail meant taking the great risk of being washed overboard or being knocked out by the waves which were pounding down and washing clean across the decks. The seas were flooding in from both sides.

Another series of big breakers quickly made my mind up. That moment I knew that the boat was lost, there was no way to sail off.

What about the liferaft? I crawled aft on all fours and freed the lashings to get it ready. But on second thoughts I decided that we stood a better chance of surviving for the moment by staying with the boat than by entrusting ourselves to the flimsy inflatable this close to the reefs. So I crawled in to join Suzanna in the cabin and quickly closed the hatch.

Everything below was a shambles. Water seemed to be finding its way in from all sides and bits of gear were being flung all over the place with each crash of the waves.

'This is it,' I remember thinking to myself. 'Keep cool, keep cool ... Do the right things.' We were now well up on the reef. Each successive wave was picking the tiny craft up in the air and slapping her down on the coral.

'We're shipwrecked,' I coolly told Suzanna, shouting above the thud of the waves, 'but everything is going to be all right.' Suzanna accepted this information calmly: either she was too stunned to react otherwise, or she'd seen it coming for so long that the situation was already quite familiar to her.

We set to rummaging around and eventually we found a flashlight that worked, and started to look for extra clothes to put on for protection from the coral. Quickly we grabbed the survival rations, emergency flares and other odds and ends, which were somehow stuffed into bags. In the pandemonium we could only hear each other by shouting.

Still more water was pouring in and cracks were appearing all around; clearly the *Kilcullen* was rapidly disintegrating and I wondered how much more she could take. Once the boat had gone we could never swim in that surf. I felt in my bones that our chances were slim, and began to look clearly at the prospect of being lost without trace and another statistic for the notorious Bermuda triangle. Yet one chance was all that we needed to survive, and on that chance we bet our lives. But in what shape would that chance come?

My hope was that the surf would wash us up on a beach where we would find ourselves high and dry the following morning; then we might sort out the damage, repair and then re-float our little yacht. But the furious sea just continued to pound us up and down on the same coral head.

As the minutes passed I was more frightened and began to wonder whether we would be given any chance to escape. 'Why me, why, why?' I kept asking, and cursing myself for dragging Suzanna into this as well. 'Hail Holy Queen, Mother of mercy . . .' Suzanna started to pray out loud. Later she had no recollection of reciting that prayer but I remember it, this moment, as clear as day.

Each blow hurt deep down with physical anguish and the mental agony that our proud trim little craft should be subjected to such a beating.

Through the astrodome I caught occasional glimpses (sensed rather than visually seen in the dark) of the outlines of cliffs. Our only hope now was to find a rock above the water mark which we could jump on to. Even to get out now to wade through the shallow water would be dangerous as the surf would pull us off our feet and smash our fragile bodies against the rocks.

Then the *Kilcullen* stopped moving across the coral and seemed to be obstructed by a black rock rising out of the foam. The pounding continued. On the undertow she was being sucked out and would then get lifted again, riding high with the wave and flung against the rugged volcanic rock.

The time had come to attempt a jump clear. It would be now or never. As soon as we opened the hatch the water came flooding in completely; everything was awash, there was no turning back. With the first lull Suzanna jumped for safety but she fell short beneath the water-line. Before she had a chance to get to her feet a wave came and washed her back into the deep. I heard her scream my name but could not see her as she disappeared from sight. I felt absolutely helpless. She was gone and it was all my fault. What strange thoughts came to me in those seconds: 'What about the funeral? No body left. How would I break the news to her family whom I'd never met? Should I jump now, to go with her and end it all?'. . .

But no, I funked the jump— I still needed time.

Then, as if by an Act of God, the *Kilcullen*'s light rounded hull performed its last heroic deed. Suzanna's head, black against the white froth, appeared between the rocks and the boat's hull, which fenced her in. As the undertow was pulling her off the rocks a second time she managed to catch a firm hold in the relative shelter of the *Kilcullen* and pull herself up out of reach before the next wave carried the boat in against her.

The next I heard was her voice calling my name through the howling wind and spray. 'I'm O.K.' she said.

I tossed her the bag of valued possessions and some other bags that came to hand before preparing to jump. Momentarily I hesitated in deciding whether to grab other valuables such as the Dancom VHF which would only take a couple of minutes to unscrew and stick in a bag. No. When it was lighter we might return to the wreckage and salvage what we could. Best to get out without losing another minute.

My jump was all the more accurate after watching Suzanna slip. The rocks were very sharp. Though I managed to get clear in the one jump, some bags got ripped open, splattering around the contents such as cameras, months of writings and so forth, to be washed away for ever. Fortunately, from within an inner bag, we saved the survival rations and flare kit.

Scarcely had we got ourselves and our rescued bits and pieces above the water's reach than there was an almighty crash. We turned to see that the keel had finally parted and watched as the *Kilcullen* capsized, breaking the mast in umpteen pieces in the process. We had been given our chance just in time.

We climbed up on to a ledge, fired a load of distress flares which apparently nobody saw, and huddled up together for protection and warmth. The wind still carried sheets of spray off the waves but at least we were safe—for the moment at any rate. Where from here we didn't know, nor did we know where we were, but there was security in each other on that big exposed rock.

In all, approximately thirty minutes had passed between our striking the coral head for the first time to this point, as I attempted to reconstruct exactly what had happened and to figure out where we were. We climbed up further on the cliff and fired another flare. As we did so we made out solid land close by which could only be Cat Island, on recollection from the chart.

But how did we get so far off course? Was there a fault in the compass? An extra magnetic variation? And what about the lighthouse on the tip of the island? Later we discovered that it was not a reliable light and had not been maintained properly, since on Independence the responsibility had passed from the British to the Bahamians. Apparently we had been caught by a cross-current, which we could only have avoided by setting more sail and increasing our speed. The current swept us on to the headland. Had we resisted its impetus for another quarter of a mile, we would have been swept clear into the Exuma Sound and open water. As it is, the currents are not correctly charted and increase greatly in storm conditions with a big sea running. A local explained to us that it changes speed and directions rapidly in this area as the water gets deep, shallow and deep again according to how the coral reefs meander. In short, I might have avoided this with better local knowledge—but the skipper must accept the consequences of his decisions.

By dawn we were cold, wet and anxious, but grateful still to be alive. The wind had abated and the seas eased somewhat. We had hoped to salvage some gear from the wreckage but were quite horrified to see that the *Kilcullen* had disappeared; all that remained were hundreds of bits of splintered wreckage scattered along fifty yards of jagged foreshore. The absolute destructive power of the sea, the coral and sharp rocks was frightening—a boat twice her size would have broken up.

From there we were relieved to find that we could make solid land without difficulty. Apart from many bruises, scrapes and cuts—some through three layers of clothing—we felt in good shape. Suzanna took consolation from noticing that the shore was littered with wrecks, including one complete aluminium hull. We speculated as to what fate they had suffered and felt deeply for them, whoever they were, alone on this desolate coast.

At least we had each other. And what a way to spend Saint Patrick's Day!

My all-American girl vowed never to spend Saint Patrick's Day with an Irishman again. However, she learned (as I too was to learn) that Never is a word that one should never use.

I put on a brave exterior, but was shaken to the core: I had lost everything in the wreck—typewriter, sextant, camera, clothing. That mashed up piece of plastic on the volcanic rock was my entire life.

That day, struggling around the coastline with one shoe between our four feet, was a difficult struggle and a long walk.

'Castaways, castaways, castaways . . .' called out an old one-legged Bahamian as he rode a mule up through the small village on the edge of the beach. There was great excitement. He had the news first from two boys who discovered us as we made our way around the shore.

It was all over. A policeman, doctor, clergyman and, it seemed, countless officials came; curiosity was great and they treated us kindly, though our grief remained private to the two of us.

After a bumpy ride on an old Bahamian Government boat, we were delivered two days later to Nassau—just like two kids who had lost their luggage. Suzanna was reluctant to call the States and cause needless alarm, while I too preferred to keep my troubles to myself and not call home. Indeed I have rarely talked or written about the shipwreck, save these words.

At Nassau Yacht Club we made new friends, who offered us everything from a hot bath and a bed to a ticket to Florida.

Suzanna and I went our separate ways: she went home to her family in Potsdam and I worked odd jobs to raise the price of an airline ticket home.

Reality was depressing. Starting from scratch again was difficult. I was unemployed and in many respects unemployable, having been turned down from several jobs. I always had some work in freelance journalism, but to get a full-time job and stability in this field was virtually impossible at the time. And what of Suzanna? The real test of love is to let a man carry you off to sea, throw you into raging surf at dead of night, and barely escape with your life, let alone your personal effects, and still to want to go on being with him. Some months later she arrived in Galway—perhaps she wanted to save me the cost of all those transatlantic telephone love calls. Then the day after being thrown out of a wedding party in the Aran Islands, where we had been stormbound on a 30ft yacht, we found ourselves running before the westerly wind back into Galway. It was a beautiful crisp sunny day. On the stern one of our crewmen played the accordion. The ocean glistened and to port the Connemara Mountains flowed while the Cliffs of Moher and Black Head loomed to starboard. As we perched in the bows, the water lapping against the side, it was truly a day for romance. I fumbled for words which came out in a jumble: 'Suzanna dear, I'm not worthy of . . . what I mean is . . . you're too good for me . . . I don't deserve you . . . will you, will you marry me . . ?'

'Yes,' Suzanna said.

I was delighted, but also horrified: I should explain that Enda O'Coineen did not, up to this time, have the slightest intention of getting married, with all that meant in complications. For a start, I was living from hand to mouth, and no father-in-law could have seen in me a solid prospect for his daughter. But such is life. Like the tide, it carries you along and there are few things more beautiful than to join the flow.

Our first year of marriage was hell. I landed a job as a furniture salesman, travelling Ireland for a time in a car in which only fresh air separated one's legs from the road. There have been better furniture salesmen and I decided that this was not the life for me.

Against most sensible advice I opted to make a career of marine journalism and to establish a boating magazine, *Ireland Afloat*. In a small market the printer, publisher and then the unfortunate journalist in that order get rewarded so, if I was going to become a marine journalist, it was important to retain some control. This magazine was to become a testimony to my stubborn nature. Besides, it kept me in touch with seamen and the sea—and with that nagging piece of unfinished business, an Atlantic crossing by inflatable.

18

Secret preparations and departure

NOT everybody thought that crossing the Atlantic in a rubber boat was the brightest of ideas, least of all those who knew my ability to jump into projects at the deep end to finish in the manure business. With our new born girl Roisin Mairead, gross registered tonnage at launch: 5lb 6oz, Suzanna was not keen on my trying further affairs with the North Atlantic but she worked with the grain: 'Sure, it was almost written into the marriage contract, you would be unbearable for the rest of our lives if I stopped you.'

On the other hand Winkie Nixon, who worked with me in *Afloat* Magazine did not believe that I really planned a second attempt—though he was told. My approach to the finance company had to be a bit subtle if I was to get a loan to buy the new inflatable.

I put the idea to him in such a way that he wouldn't believe me. With no security and no prospect of insurance, one could not expect a rational Bank Manager to lend the money—however it was important not to tell him lies. 'It's a grand boat,' said I to Mr Lowther. 'You could even cross the Atlantic in it and I might give it a try.' He let this pass, and could not deny having been told.

Rather than go off in a blaze of publicity, the last thing I wanted was for the voyage to be seen as a stunt. It was a private settling of accounts between myself and my destiny. If the preparations did not work out as planned I wanted the option of being able to 'abort the mission'. I was mindful of the tragic case of Donald Crowhurst, who announced to the public that he intended racing around the world when he was not ready. In the end he felt compelled to go because of the publicity, and ended up taking his own life.

It seemed only natural to call the new inflatable *Kilcullen III* but this time there would be no elaborate naming ceremony. The final delivery of *Kilcullen III* to me in Wales marked the end of several weeks planning all the details and making preparations. I had crossed the Irish Sea from Dublin to collect it.

Seeing it from a distance on a trailer for the first time I marvelled at how small and frail it looked. 'Is this really it? What have you let yourself in for!' I muttered. Though roughly the same length as the original *Kilcullen,* this new one from Humber Inflatables had a rigid hull and a self-righting frame; this frame had an inflatable tube mounted on top which was linked to a compressed air bottle lashed to the stern. The idea was that on capsize I would open the air bottle, inflate the bag and the boat would come upright. There was no such system on *Kilcullen I.*

For driving power this time it was my intention to get across as quickly as was physically possible. Therefore I had obtained a 55 h.p. Suzuki outboard motor and a 9.9 h.p. back-up model. To supplement that, I had a sailing rig fairly similar to *Kilcullen I*'s since there was no way that it would be physically possible to carry fuel for that distance.

Otherwise both inflatables were fairly similar, each having a tent-like cover, though *Kilcullen III*'s was much better designed and made by Downer's in Dun Laoghaire out of plastic instead of canvas.

Back on Holyhead quayside as we prepared to make *Kilcullen III*'s maiden voyage of some sixty miles to Dublin, a casual observer gave me a knowing wink and remarked: 'There was a crazy Irishman here some years ago with an inflatable just like this. Said he almost crossed the Atlantic in it. The navy had rescued him and he left from this very spot to cross the Irish Sea.' 'Must have been a right nut case,' I muttered. I hadn't the heart to admit to being that crazy Irishman—nor did I want to cope with all the banter that would follow. Even Michael Finnegan, who was coming with me on the delivery trip across the Irish Sea, had not been told what the final intentions for the boat were.

With Customs cleared, we made the crossing without incident—though on arrival in Dun Laoghaire we raised a few eyebrows, having taken such a small craft across the Irish Sea.

I had thought nothing of it.

Over the next six weeks, I experimented with different rigs and took the inflatable on trials—ostensibly the inflatable was earmarked for marine photography. One trial involved loading up to capacity with the special inflatable fuel tanks imported from France; happily it all went well.

My plan this time was to set out from Halifax, Nova Scotia, previously my last port of departure. By the end of June I had the inflatable and gear carefully packed away in a container loaded on a ship bound for Halifax via Scotland while I prepared to fly out ten days later.

This gap was the first opportunity to really stop and think what I had let myself into. For the previous six months I had been doing such an excellent public-relations job on Suzanna to persuade her that the voyage would not involve much risk, I almost began to believe it myself. Nonetheless I took time out to make a will—though I had no idea then that most of the life insurance policies would have been void because of the nature of the trip.

Before going to Halifax myself, I needed to stop in New York and Boston to complete my preparations. In New York I was checked into the New York Yacht Club by a member friend, Don Graul. The club is, of course, associated with serious yacht racing, the sport of millionaires, and not least the 12-meter America's Cup Defenders, those greyhounds of the yacht-racing scene, so I kept a bit quiet about my rubber boat and my proposed voyage. Luckily my suit of clothes was just smart enough to avoid sticking out like a sore thumb in such well heeled company. I even had a shine on my shoes.

Don Graul of course took me to the special room built to hold the America's Cup. After a hundred years and some two dozen challenges, the Club finally lost the Cup to the Australians last time round, but from the talk around the bar, they plan to get it back at the next opportunity. Meanwhile, other paintings and models have managed to hide the hole.

With 3,000 assorted members this is reckoned to be the most exclusive Yacht Club in the world. And good luck to them, though their library is fabulous. If they're any good they'll have this book in it as well!—I can just see it—the Unsinkable *Kilcullen* inflatable boat story alongside that of the Vanderbilt Yachts or

Sir Thomas Lipton. What, people might enquire, has the world come to!

Despite the fact that you'll never find any yachts out in front of the club, being located smack in the middle of New York, members are all sailing folk though 'One or two that are not really the sailing type have slipped in from time to time,' an old gentleman explained at the bar. As I was about to be on my way, after sharing the hospitality of Don Graul and his charming wife Rebecca, she told me: 'You're very different to many of Don's macho-type yachting friends.' Was this the ultimate compliment, I wondered.

In Boston I made a quick call to my old friend Mike Connolly, the man with no hands who saw me off from Boston eight years previously. Again it was like going back in time, and rather than stay, I moved on quickly to Halifax. It took over a day to track down my old friend Bill Buckley, a wonderful character. Since meeting him last in the Virgin Islands he had been divorced and had gone gloriously bankrupt in St John's, Newfoundland having been squeezed out by a big multinational in the business he established. By now he was managing a big beer pub 'The Green Dory', and was also managing some apartment blocks with his brothers. His apartment was on the ground floor and I was not long there and had opened the blinds when he shouted: 'Quick, quick, close the blinds, I make an easy target!' Apparently somebody had been trying to kill him. I was not long in discovering who and why.

Bill has a heart of gold and quite honestly I could not understand why anybody who really knew him would want to kill him. He was adventurous—given the opportunity, he would have come the whole way with me; above all else, he really identified with the adventure aspect of it all.

Staying in Bill's apartment, though, was, as I discovered, an adventure in itself. King Billy as I called him, after William of Orange in Irish history, was mad about sex. A real macho woman charmer 'soft yet tough as they come'; the ladies seem to love him and of late he informed me that he had never had it so good.

'They love it man, they can't get enough of it,' said Bill as he showed me his bedroom complete with his king-size water-bed. I simply could not believe the tackle he had bolted to either ends of the bed to tie the ladies down. To boot, there was a large block and tackle hanging out of the ceiling. For sheer devilment, with no ulterior motives in so far as I could gather, he has a curtain at the back of his bedroom opening to a small secret room where sometimes he mounted a video infra-red camera to film the proceedings.

From my journal of July 14th I wrote: 'Bill is staying with another girl tonight. It's almost impossible to keep up with all his ladies, most of whom have superb bodies and sharp minds. That reminds me, it's Suzanna's birthday on July 17th, must send some flowers. It's O.K. for Bill to do what he wants but I'm a one-woman man.'

In fact that night I got to sleep on the water-bed which was welcome after the couch, but I got a shock around 3 a.m. when Bill arrived suddenly back in the apartment, visibly shaken. He hadn't mentioned that the girl he was staying with was married and her husband came home by surprise, drunk. The husband's hobby is guns so Bill decided not to stick around, but escaped through several back gardens.

The ship eventually docked at Halifax with the container holding the *Kilcullen*. When clearing Customs to get the inflatable out of the container terminal the Customs official remembered my trip of eight years previously. Everything went like clock-work. A top-up of air and the *Kilcullen* was launched. One of the dockers recalled a man who had arrived there previously with a 20-foot submarine of 'revolutionary' design to cross the North Atlantic. 'After a month he got smart and shipped it back home in the container. If you've any sense you'll do the same,' the docker added.

On motoring across Halifax harbour, the last thing in the world I expected was to be pulled in for speeding on the water. To complicate matters with the water policeman, the *Kilcullen* had no registration marks of any description. This sent a shiver down my spine; if the Coast Guard wanted to stop me going there was little I could do. As I rapidly made my excuses to the policeman my mind was quickly turning over ways to give the officials the slip.

The weather was unsettled and I delayed going; there always seemed to be something still left unfinished on the boat. Finally a favourable weather window arrived, and with it the actual moment of departure. As on previous attempts, I had last-minute cold feet. Here I was, back at my old game of dicing with death. Bill Buckley offered me a light-weight bag, totally sealed (except for the head) to keep as a survival suit. Its normal function was a disposable container for corpses. He said that he could get it from an undertaker friend who had loaned him one once and Bill claimed, it was just the ticket.

An undertaker is generally recognized as the 'last man to let you down'; even so, I was not sure that I wanted such an object on board.

Now, fully loaded, it was time to go. It was a wet and cold July morning. A quick telephone call home to Suzanna, flowers for Bill's mother, who had fed me and given me mooring space, and the *Kilcullen* with her apprehensive skipper cast off. We punched out into the short nasty chop and headed for the open sea. Fog descended to hide the dark headlands, drizzle merged sea and sky, but the compass told us which way Ireland lay— or so I thought.

19

'*Never' is a word you should never use*

NOT far out from Halifax harbour the waves were already giving the *Kilcullen* a rough ride. As I watched the steering compass, a big green 'un surged up and tore it clean off its mountings. I found it undamaged and refixed it—but I had been warned!

I set course north-east, well clear of land . . . or so I thought, until an hour or two later a different feel to the swell which started to break alerted me to danger: in the fog I had stumbled into a series of reefs. I could not see them, but the sound of the water breaking on them told me enough. I motored out of there as fast as possible, and not a little shaken up. What had gone wrong with my navigation? I had a little satellite navigator which should have helped, but it was already out of order. I was left puzzling, until the following day I got some lines of position with coastal radio beacons, using the old reliable Seafarer RDF, and had to conclude that my compass had a consistent error of over fifteen degrees, which could only have come from the knock it received as we left harbour.

I was a little older and wiser than on my first attempt, but the fact remained—the Atlantic had not changed, and the new *Kilcullen* was no roomier than the old. Despite the physical training programme with which I'd prepared for the voyage, life on board was difficult, uncomfortable and cramped. After allowing for the tubes, all the equipment, provisions and fuel, my living quarters—if they could be described as such—measured about three feet square.

My plan was to sweep well outside the coastal traffic and come in to St John's, Newfoundland, to gain easting.

On the second day out the seas mounted as the wind picked up from the south to about twenty knots. The *Kilcullen's* movement made me seasick. I seldom get it badly—a lot depends on diet and the type of boat movement. In this instance, I think that it was the tension and pressures of the previous weeks, getting ready practically and spiritually, which caused it. Seasickness is something you learn to handle; the important thing is not letting it affect your reactions and logic, or you can be in real trouble, especially when alone or skippering a boat.

The days which followed were boring, cold and monotonous as I motored on through night and day using the auto pilot, seeing virtually nothing in the fog. Again, as in the first *Kilcullen* voyage, I had to adjust to the cold-water temperature of the Labrador current and I longed for the Gulf Stream. While sleeping I would slow down for fear of being run over by a coastal steamer or fishing boat. The *Kilcullen* had a radar reflector with a radius of about eighteen inches but, being so low down in the water, it always risked getting lost in the sea-clutter.

For this voyage I kept a log sealed in three plastic bags but still it managed to get wet. Later, after making a landfall, I was to need a hair-dryer on it before I could make out what I'd written. Entries over this period are sparse, just a record of navigational points.

July 19th. Wind is building from the south-west. The fog has cleared, there is a big swell now and a new weather system seems to be moving in. There is something in the air, I don't like the feel of things.

That night it blew up a storm. In the dark I could scarcely see the waves as they came toppling down on us, but the noise of breaking water was frightening enough. Rather than take the risk of capsize I let the *Kilcullen* fill with water to act as ballast, dropped all sail and cut the engine to run off before the storm. With the helm lashed, I huddled up in a ball on one of the tubes forward. Using isometric exercises which involved tensioning and relaxing the muscles, I managed to stay warm as the hurricane raged through the night. There was no way to describe the strength of the wind, save to say that it was fearful to hear it shrieking across the wavetops.

'This is it,' I said to myself after some hours of this and decided that if I pulled through I'd also pull out and quietly forget about the Atlantic attempt. If it was like this only a few days out, I could not see myself surviving conditions like this for a month or more.

Storms do eventually peter out, thank God, and this one did just before I reached snapping point. Later I was to learn that we had come through the tail end of Hurricane Anna which had altered course—no wonder I imagined it was coming after me!

The *Kilcullen* and her skipper bounced out of it both in one piece and as the sun rose towards noon, I got under way in better spirits and with second thoughts about pulling out.

The following morning land lay before me and I put in to what turned out to be the French island of St Pierre, off the southern coast of Newfoundland. Perhaps it was due to the fact that I had been expelled from school and missed the geography classes that covered this area, I don't know, but certainly I had never heard of the place. A large French flag flew over the harbour.

St Pierre is noted for its shipwrecks, which have contributed to the islanders' prosperity, in addition to what they earned from fishing and smuggling. The main population of about 5,000 live on St Pierre, some five miles long. They speak French, use French currency and tend to be educated in France.

The *Kilcullen* slipped quietly into the small-boat area of the harbour, and nobody seemed to take much notice other than a casual Customs official, who was very surprised to discover that I'd been out in Hurricane Anna, as he conversed with me in a broken English and sign language.

I then made my way up the main street to the Hotel Robert with a fierce thirst and longing for a hot bath. As I waited in the bar for the bath-water to heat up, a 1920s style trilby hanging on the wall caught my attention. I was told that it was once worn by the gangster Al Capone: it was here that he used to stay during the height of the Prohibition era, keeping out of the eye of the Law as he looked after his smuggling interests.

From the hotel keeper, who luckily could speak English, I

learnt something about these islands. With the invasion of the Falklands by Argentina in the spring of 1982, this French island archipelago came into the news as well: Canadian papers were quick to draw parallels between the South Atlantic war and Canada's claims over the islands. In particular, with the expanding oil interests and the 200-mile fishing zones, these islands presented a great deal of potential for conflict, being only twelve miles off the coast of Newfoundland. Nonetheless, the islanders did not seem too concerned: 'The Canadians are one thing, the Argentinians quite another,' seemed the general relaxed opinion.

The islands were first discovered in the early 1500s by the Portuguese explorer, João Alvarez Fagundes. When he landed, on the feast day of St Ursula, he named the little archipelago 'The Eleven Thousand Virgins'. It was Jacques Cartier who claimed the islands for the King of France on the return trip from his second voyage of discovery to the St Lawrence River. When he stopped at St Pierre he found a number of Frenchmen already using the harbour. Since then, the islands changed hands several times.

Well rested, I set out to take a long walk around St Pierre, which looked rather decayed. One thing that I couldn't help noticing was the number of old broken down lawn-mowers, when there was so little grass in evidence. But then it started to pour with rain so I stopped in at a barber shop I was passing at the time, for to have a hair-cut would be a good way to help pass the time. The hair-cut took two hours, for the barber spoke good English and enjoyed a long chat.

Jacques the barber spoke of the 674 shipwrecks recorded on the islands since 1800, with many more un-recorded. As it was close to the main shipping lane up the Gulf of St Lawrence from South America and Europe, many ships came this way only to be wrecked on the rocks in the fog. Of course the increasing use of radar during and after the Second World War radically reduced the fog risk and thereby virtually wiped out an important part of the islanders' economy. Miquelon suffered particularly, and its population has now dropped to a quarter of what it was in the heyday of plundering wrecks.

One wreck, Jacques told me, had landed 1,200 cows on the islands, all in fair health and mooing lustily. The horned cattle proceeded to run wild over the island, scaring the living daylights out of the unwary natives, who boarded themselves up in their houses.

But what about all the old lawn-mowers?

I asked Jacques as he carefully plucked my hairs. The barber's eyes lit up. They came from the last major wreck we had, he explained. It was a German freighter in the 1960s; its radar was on the blink and the ship wanted to take refuge here while it effected repairs—but the ship foundered close to the harbour. Once it was determined that the ship could not be saved, the islanders had the full cargo-load of lawn mowers and other goods cleared from the ship inside 24 hours.

With a damp and foggy climate, the islanders are in decline, though great efforts are being made to attract tourists. It is the fishing trade that keeps them going, and the prospect of a big oil strike. The place is chiefly noted as a centre for great rum-running and alcohol smuggling during America's Prohibition period between 1920s and 1930s. The French could never understand Prohibition, but they certainly made lots of money out of it.

In addition to Al Capone and other gangsters who frequented the island, it was for a while the home of the famous Irishman Bill McCoy. Known as 'the real McCoy' by his customers along the New England coast, he stood out for always smuggling and delivering the best liquor and there was never any watering down – or so the legend has it.

Finally, rested, cleaned up and with a neat hair-cut at last, I set out once again for St John's, Newfoundland, some 200 miles away. But not before I had bought fuel at the garage beside where the *Kilcullen* was berthed. The proprietor sold not only petrol but also beer a-plenty—and he turned out to be one of his own best customers and insisted that I have several drinks with him before fueling the *Kilcullen;* I can't say I minded. To pay him there was no rate of exchange handy, so I had to convert Irish pounds into U.S. dollars into Canadian dollars into French francs. (The face on the note, I told my friend, is always solemn, but on the £50 note it has a great big smile—a pity I didn't have one to show him.)

Through the beautiful early morning sun and perfect visibility, unusual for this part of the world, St Pierre disappeared behind me below the horizon. Everything was just perfect, as I drove the *Kilcullen* at twenty knots over the glass-like surface. I encountered dolphins who followed the *Kilcullen* for a time, something which was to become a feature of the entire crossing. For hours they would follow the *Kilcullen*, criss-crossing the bow playfully and talking to me in their high-pitched squeak.

There were plenty of sharks too, and they acted playful as well. With the hard bottom this time by comparison with the 1977 crossing, I felt greater security. In terms of marine life, this area on the Grand Banks is very rich and teeming with activity. The Irish name for the area, which has strong historical links with Ireland, is far more appropriate as 'Talamh an Eisc', The Land of the Fish.

Some twenty miles off Cape St Mary, the final major headland before Cape Race on the southern tip of Newfoundland, I encountered several schools of whales. A whale is always a whale of an animal and takes up plenty of space, but these I saw were relatively small. It was their noise and smell which left more of an impression on me than their size. They make a sort of high-pressure gushing sound, and they smell of fish, and not very fresh fish. On the surface you know they've been around when you see lots of small dead fish floating on oily water: the whales just swim along with their mouths wide open through shoals of fish, gobble them up, and pass the rejects up through their spouts.

Initially I kept my distance from the whales, but then, feeling more adventurous, and with the powerful Suzuki outboard to let me back away from them in a hurry, I started to follow them and take some photographs having great sport through the waves. Unlike the whalers in their whaleboats, I had no mother ship to return to, but as I had no harpoon either, the whales and the *Kilcullen* were not at war.

The whales tended to move in pairs; one moment I would see their heads and enormous bodies breaking the surface for air followed by their tails and then they would dive into the depths, to resurface about five minutes later. Their sheer beauty and grace captivated me, and as I followed them, some lines from the whaling song *Greenland* went round in my head: the whale had capsized the whaling brig drowning her crew:—

Now the losing of them fine jolly men
   it grieved the captain sore;

25. (*Right*) and
26. (*below*)
Kilcullen (III).
Tuning up off
St John's,
Newfoundland.
(*Daily Express*)

27. (*Above*) and 28. (*below*) *Kilcullen (III)*. Sea trials.

29. Sea trials and sail balance. *(Ireland Afloat)*

30. *Kilcullen (III)*. The cockpit. *(Daily Express)*

31. Guest of Guinness (being a good customer) at the
Boat Show – with a fellow racing man, Richard Branson.

32. High and dry. *Kilcullen (III)* in Piccadilly, London, as I receive
the Black Bush Whiskey Award for Outstanding Human
Endeavour. *(Press Association)*

But the losing of that fine sperm whale—
   Well it grieved him ten times more.
Brave boys, brave boys . . .

The whales were big enough, as I say, but next to the first
iceberg I saw floating along they looked like tadpoles. The iceberg
appeared as a small island on the horizon. 'Funny,' I thought;
'there should not be an island there,' so I checked my chart,
fearing that the *Kilcullen*'s navigation was all wrong. Well, no,
it could never be an island so it had to be an iceberg. Even going
flat out under Suzuki-power, it took an hour to reach it—it lay
some 25 miles off. First the berg was like an egg on the horizon,
then it seemed like an ice-cream and then, from another angle,
it looked like a Spanish church. At this stage the slanting evening
sun lit the berg, which reacted like a prism, breaking the rays
up into every colour of the rainbow. Closer to, it appeared like
a giant iced cake, reminding me of my wedding cake and good
wife at home in Ireland.

Beside the iceberg the *Kilcullen* was tiny. The main part rose
sheer out of the water, a hundred feet or more. Then the
submerged part of the berg kept surfacing at intervals in ledges
and pinnacles of ice as much as a hundred yards away from the
main ice cliffs.

The iceberg made a growling sound, and in addition there
was the constant noise of water flowing, like a waterfall: we
were now late July, it was very far south and thawing at a furious
rate, which accounted for the waterfalls. I went alongside to
touch it. Being the first iceberg I've ever seen close-up, it left a
marked impression. It had a magical eerie quality, radiating a
cold beauty which would send sculptors into ecstasy.

I could have spent hours watching it but the evening was
advancing rapidly and it was time to get moving for St John's,
where I arrived in the darkness some hours later.

I spent four days in St John's, gearing up to take the ultimate
plunge. I couldn't help secretly hoping that a bad weather forecast
would give me an excuse to linger in the safety of the harbour,
but in fact the forecast was good, so there was nothing for it
but to cast off and motor out into the ocean, which, I felt it in
my bones, was not going to let a cheeky little rubber boat sail
across it without punishment. Like a lead bullet the full enormity

of what lay ahead struck home. Again I would love to have said that I was brave and undisturbed and not afraid of the Atlantic but no, my love-hate affair with this stretch of ocean was once again being put to the test.

It was 1700 hours, 25 July 1985.

20

Cold and misery

CANADA'S eastern outpost disappeared astern into the evening gloom. Darkness approached and, as I motored on into the night, it was cold and wet, penetrating even the three layers of clothes and two layers of oilskins. I motored, for the sooner I was clear of the cold Labrador current and into the Gulf Stream, the sooner conditions should improve.

At times, as the seas started to build, the *Kilcullen* felt more like a submarine than a boat, as reflected in the log:

> Day 1, 25th July. I am seriously worried about sinking! I may have to dump some fuel. The waves are getting fairly big and the small engine is not quick enough to drive the boat ahead to stop the waves coming over the stern. It would be very embarrassing to have to be rescued at this stage.

In fact, when we were stationary, the waves actually flowed over the stern, such was the load, so I had to keep moving. This was a calculated risk since my estimated load of 2,500 lb was fifty per cent more than the manufacturer's recommended maximum. Fifteen hundred pounds of this was in petrol, which I'd taken on at St John's, the idea being to burn it off quickly in the push to get to the Gulf Stream.

Another problem was the fumes as I tried to rest. Since two-thirds of the limited area was covered with the inflatable fuel tanks, the only place to put my head down was on top of the tanks; this brought on a headache and a mild form of seasickness.

163

Likewise, since the small 9.9 h.p. could not keep the overladen boat going fast enough before the waves to stop her from filling, I had to run the large 55 h.p. engine at displacement speed—ploughing through the waves instead of going fast enough to get up and over them—and this was not as efficient as planned. Although this motor was most useful on the run up along the Canadian coast, at one stage I had considered replacing it with a 25 h.p. for this main crossing. But as a single-handed sailor without a regular support team I had to rule this out.

> Day 2, 26th July. Good day's run, 192.6 miles, not bad for the first 24 hours. There is a large iceberg to port; this makes me nervous tonight.

While the wind remained at about 25 to 30 knots from the south-west, with a big sea running, this was very good progress, though fuel consumption was more than expected. The weather remained cold and the sun was virtually absent. I was going further north than planned because of the south in the wind; in these stormy conditions it was best to keep the seas on the quarter or to run off before them. Navigation should have been less of a problem than last time, for I had a sophisticated piece of equipment—a satellite navigator. Had it worked, it might have been quite a help, though I wasn't too worried yet, being well away from land.

What bothered me more at the moment was never being able to get properly warm; being so close to the sea and cold water, it was a constant struggle to keep my blood temperature a few degrees above that of the sea.

> Day 3, 27th July. Day's run 209 miles. Great Stuff. It blew stink for a while last night, but wind eased off again. Got an awful shock in the darkness. Was going along slowly on autopilot and sleeping when there was a gentle thud and scraping sound. The *Kilcullen* had run straight into an iceberg. Woke with a start. There it was rising straight into the air, but I just bounced off gently and got away as quickly as possible from the cold which it radiated.

> Day 4, 28th July. Day's run 155 miles. What an awful

day—and night! At the rate things are going it looks like being a survival battle to the bitter end. Oh how this damned North Atlantic can be cruel on mind and body. Looks as if we're getting closer to the Stream. Got the sails set the first time. It was going well until the wind got up to gale force and everything had to come down to ride it out.   The mast support is being ripped out of place, must do something to secure it. After darkness I was convinced that the mainsail and yard were gone because of poor lashing—fortunately just one clew rope held and I saved it just in time. Waves continue to swamp the boat, though the water does not seem as cold.   Why, why, why? You had everything going and you had to talk yourself into this silly voyage. You stupid fool, Enda!

Day 5, 29th July. Day's run: 84 miles, Oops—some dolphins cutting past as I start to write. Am being pushed quite far north. This is worrying.

While the nights continued to be cold and miserable, each 24-hour period seemed to bring its own mini crisis. During a period that day when I had the sails up they backed to push the *Kilcullen* in the other direction. My usual remedy was to start the engine to power the boat back onto course but, while I was busy sorting out the electrics to do this, the water came flooding in over the stern. The small motor now would not start and before I knew it the boat was under two feet of water.

At this stage everything was getting wet and despite my layers of thermal underwear, clothes and a drysuit under the two layers of oilskins, I remained cold—the wind-chill factor being the greatest threat.

Almost to spite everything I was trying to do, yet another frontal system and depression moved in, generating gale-force winds for over ten hours. With no sail up it was sheer misery riding out the storm, but there was little to do except grin and bear it.

Day 6, 30th July. Progress is slow. The weather has settled again. I've managed to work a little further south and was rewarded by spotting a ship at 1130hrs. Her name was something like this: *Liaxfoss*. To my surprise, though steaming past about three quarters of a mile away, they did not spot me.

'Calling passing ship, passing ship, this is inflatable *Kilcullen, Kilcullen, Kilcullen,* do you read me, do you read me? Over,' I called out a couple of times. Then I received a reply in broken English. 'This is *Liaxfoss, Liaxfoss* calling *Kilcullen, Kilcullen,* where are you?'

I simply could not believe my luck and though I could see the ship as clear as day it took some conversation, and a description of where the *Kilcullen* was in relation to them, before they spotted the orange inflatable. After that I tried to make more conversation with the radio operator since I was hungry for human company but no, he seemed very businesslike and not the chatty sort, although he did kindly give me a position and agreed to pass a message home to say that everything was O.K. Later that day, Suzanna got a call from Reykjavik in Iceland, reporting the *Kilcullen*'s position.

The position report, while welcome, was disturbing in that my navigation was nearly 100 miles out. The sea-water had evidentally taken its toll on the satellite navigator so there was no option but to get out the old plastic sextant and pray for some sun to give me a sun-sight.

After my encounter with the ship the weather began to deteriorate yet again and the seas started to build once more, adding to the ocean turbulence not yet settled from the previous gale. From then on my log entries became very sparse after I wrote:

Day 7, 31st July. The wind built up from the south during the night and graduated to a rip roaring gale at dawn. Now it has calmed off a bit and this log is one of the few remaining dry objects on board (sealed in three plastic bags). It is a struggle to write each day but to keep track of my position and retain sanity it is critical.

The seas were very confused through the blow and scared the living daylights out of me. One wave nearly capsized us while another swamped the boat completely. By running at low speed under motor, I managed to keep ahead of them.

It was an awful morning and an awful day. This is a

living nightmare. A storm is O.K. if you have a sound boat under you; but one that flexes with every wave is a bit much. At least most yachts are automatically self-righting. I am very worried, on edge, progress is slow and the petrol is low. I pray to God that everything will stay together.

This entire voyage is silly. Suzanna would probably lose her nut if she realized the risk I am constantly under— living by my wits. This Atlantic is a crazy unpredictable ocean. I'll never beat it but sure as all hell I'm going to get to the other side. There is no option.

Once again the *Kilcullen* was blown towards the turbulent edge of the Gulf Stream as the wind howled with increased fury, piling the waves high. Each massive wall of water was a threat. With an occasional surging wave breaking over the *Kilcullen,* my whole world would become a gurgling mass of confused water, which was sucked away only for the next one to pour in over me in a never-ending procession.

It was the rogue wave that I feared most. This is one that towers above the rest. In stormy waters it might be a matter of hours before the right combination of circumstances in wind and current will give birth to it. I could handle it if I was alert and saw it coming; the trick was to boost power from the big engine which miraculously kept going and enabled me to accelerate away, otherwise I would most certainly have been capsized before this.

It is impossible to tell the height of waves; from a tiny craft the wave may look like a mountain on the move, and people speak of sixty-foot waves but even in the worst storms in the open ocean, they're unlikely to top 25 or 35 feet as a rule— though the rogue wave can indeed be three times that size.

While I had seen little sea life in the storms and since leaving the Grand Banks of Newfoundland, around that time I noticed out of the corner of my eye something odd breaking in the water ahead. It sent a shiver up my spine even before I made out precisely what it was.

Since most whales normally glide along the surface of the water between dives, when you see their enormous tails, you rarely see more than a fraction of their bodies. This whale I saw, which could have been a sperm but I'm not sure, must have been caught unawares by a large wave. He literally fell out of it and momentarily, frozen in time, I saw the entire mammal's body, from head to tail as it fell through the air between the surging spray, crest and bottom of the wave—not unlike those rare photographs of surfers 'tubing it' between waves.

That body was enormous as it flew through the air; twenty yards closer and the *Kilcullen* could have been smashed to pieces. It disappeared as quickly as it appeared out of the wave, but remained long enough to be engrained on my mind and put my heart sideways in an already unsteady stomach.

The waves of that storm were as big as I had ever seen in all my life, and that included the 1979 Fastnet storm and a small hurricane off Bermuda from the deck of a well found yacht; I have never seen seas bigger, nor do I ever wish to again: their power is truly frightening. The waves were awkward and clumsy, running together from odd angles—they were brought about by a change in wind direction and the turbulent edge of the Stream.

Nothing remained save to go into the drastic survival mode, which once again involved letting the boat fill with water, for I had burnt up most of the petrol ballast which had kept me so low in the water on leaving St John's. While risking exposure, with the waves going through the boat and me rather than sliding away, at least this way a capsize would be much less likely and I would not need to handle the boat with such concentration in running off before the waves.

Then it came: I could see, or rather hear it coming but at that instant I was caught in transition, between the two storm-riding modes. First there was a rumbling which grew into a thunderous roar. Then I was pitched into the old nightmare I had lived through eight years ago off the west coast of Ireland. Water came tumbling from every direction, day became night, I was being flung about like clothes in a washing machine. As it was happening to me I couldn't quite believe it. Almost instantly I was struggling inside the upturned boat and the roar was disappearing fast, oblivious to my fate. There was a sort of eerie silence, a lull before the next angry breaking crest.

Eight years ago my primitive self-righting plan did not work; would the new system, using a compressed air cylinder, work any better?

There was little time to panic as I gasped for air trapped under the boat and moved fast to put the emergency plan into action in a cautious, calculating way.

As I crawled back along the tubes under the transom board onto the upturned bottom, I'll never forget the sensation of making it into daylight again and the cutting wind, as I automatically pulled the rip-cord to the large air-bag mounted on the so-called relf-righting frame. This was the ultimate test.

Nothing happened. Or so it seemed, as the tube seemed to take an eternity to inflate. The reality was closer to a minute before the *Kilcullen* popped up the right side and I crawled in back over the transom. I kept the boat full of water, the storm raged on and I was both exhausted and shaken.

My food and water were in sealed plastic bags and containers. I was relieved to see that most of them were still there after the capsize. Each time the storm looked like blowing itself out and I started to relax, the wind would pipe up from another direction and the torment would continue. The Atlantic intended this time to destroy me. Would I ever set eyes again on land? Would I find myself easily persuaded that any low-lying cloud bank was land? How long could I hold myself together?

Since there was no refill for the large self-righting bag I left it inflated. There was a great deal of windage but at least the bag would automatically right the *Kilcullen* if she capsized again— or so I hoped.

Time crawled. Any movement aggravated the salt sores which were constantly wet. Attending to my personal plumbing, normally disposed of with a bucket since it was too dangerous to do it directly over the side, involved seven zips (eight if you include my fly zipper) and was simply not possible, so after a few days it was primitive and animal-like as the zips remained closed.

Following a makeshift repair to the mast, which broke in the capsize, I was able to get moving again two days later, by August 4th—initially under sail since the engines would not start. Water kept flowing freely in over the stern, and it was a case of ten buckets out and nine buckets in as I bailed furiously for over an hour. This is when I learnt the truth of the dictum that there is nothing more effective than a frightened man with a bucket!

The two-odd hours of sunshine around noon were like manna

from heaven as I attempted to strip. My right foot was quite sore and it came as a shock when my boot woud not come off, though eventually the deed was accomplished with great pain. Was it an infection from a small cut? Was it gangrene? Would I lose a foot? On board I had a fairly comprehensive first-aid kit which included stitching material, freeze spray to stop severe bleeding and so forth, but how could I handle this? O'Coineen had no plans to go through life on one foot!

Eventually I deduced the possible cause to be the rubber seal on the suit, which could be stopping or affecting circulation to my foot. Beside the painfully slow and awkward aspect of removing the drysuit and layers of clothing, the smell was foul and my body was filthy after so many days imprisoned in them. Never before had I sunk so low.

I stripped naked and turned into one big goose pimple in the icy cold wind as I jumped into the ocean—with a safety harness lashed around my chest. After a quick 40-second scrub I was out again, and gratefully pulled on some dry clothing which had miraculously survived the capsize in a sealed bag. I was a new man and the psychological uplift was great. I then massaged my foot to get the swelling down, while discarding the smelly drysuit.

Things were starting to look up and my sleeping bag was even drying out quickly in the sunshine. Even when damp, this bag had proved invaluable as it provided insulation in survival conditions. But a large wave had come and swept it away, just when I had been looking forward to my first comfortable sleep for some days. I recovered it as it was tied to the boat, but having to go without it in the meantime was depressing.

Day 12, 5th August. So hard to find anything to write with. [All the pens on board had stopped working.] This pencil is literally only $1\frac{1}{2}$ inches long. The log is also bending like pulp while the boat had been flexing in the waves.

I'm worried about my mast repair holding up and the symptoms of an ulcer from the constant tension and worry.

At this stage, with the constant wear, chafe on the tubes was a great concern and every day I had what I called 'Chafe watch'.

A small rope rubbing for an hour or two would not make any difference, but after a day or two it could easily wear a hole. One time the anchor, which was lashed to the aft frame, nearly wore a hole right through before I got to it.

By the following day I was swamped again (drying-out sleeping bag and all) in another blow; but my spirits rose that evening when I got the engines started after clearing the water from the fuel system. Having feared the worst, I was delighted to hear the engines running again. With solid-state electronics, the modern Suzuki engines came out trumps.

By this time I was over two weeks out of St John's and, following losses in the storm, had to introduce stricter rationing. Though progress was good the going was still very tough and it had not warmed up as I had hoped. Still without the sleeping bag, it was difficult to stay warm enough to sleep for more than half an hour—then sometimes I worried that I would go beyond the point of waking up.

By using isometric exercises—as far as I could with so many layers of clothes and salt sores—I would warm up, tire myself out and drop off to sleep. However about half an hour later I would wake up cold and would have to go through the same routine again.

Day 16, 9th August. I'm drinking champagne and eating chicken curry—fresh from can! It's amazing what 10 hours of fair wind and a little sunshine can do following the gale which raged for the last twenty hours.

I'm lonely, wet and cold. Still a long way to go.

I had a bottle of whiskey out of which I would take a small sup each evening—this was the absolute maximum since lone drinking under such pressure is potentially lethal. However as a sort of psychological carrot, I had a small bottle of champagne taped to one frame to celebrate the half way mark. After two glasses, my head was in a spin and I started to shout and roar and sing; fortunately there was nobody for hundreds of miles in either direction to hear all of this.

21

Landfall and bliss

BY NOW I was barely doing more than existing. It was only by escaping into my thoughts, escaping out of my body as it were, that I managed to keep going. From where I sat there was only one alternative to succeeding and that was to die in the attempt, so I could not think of failing.

Though I am not a particularly religious person, God came a lot into my thoughts. I thought of him with the power to raise tempests, and the power to walk on the water and to make the rough sea flat, as Jesus had done on the Sea of Galilee. Maybe the thought was put into my head by telepathy: I was unaware that by this time half the womenfolk of my home town were busy saying rosaries and offering novenas for the lone sailor. Well, I was certainly giving them something to pray about! I longed to make contact with shore to say that everything was O.K. so as not to cause any unnecessary worry, but all my communications facilities were knocked out in the capsize.

One by one, I started to cross off the days. I finished off the last few remaining novels on board. These represented another form of escape and, though the paperbacks were wet through, by peeling off each page and throwing it over the side when finished, I managed some good reads.

At this stage what Chay Blyth calls 'Mental plonk' set in. By this I mean that the mind, cut off from all outside influences, lost any relative perspective. If, for example, I decided to make an adjustment to the sail, I might sit for an hour and then suddenly find myself doing it. It was a peculiar sort of delayed reaction. Food, or rather the lack of it, was also a constant preoccupation as I wrote in the log:

Day 20, 13th August. I'm getting hungry. This rationing is mentally very demanding. I must fight it and resist the temptation to eat everything now. I dream of a juicy steak, fresh pineapple and chocolate, lots and lots of it.

I'm inclined to talk out loud to myself and hear other people's voices at night around the boat. Individual conversations going on while I sleep—that sort of thing.

Having been through several single-handed voyages previous to this, each time not wishing to go single-handed again, my observations in the log entry above are not all that unusual and represent experiences that several other single-handers have gone through. In short, by this time, I should have been used to this sort of thing.

I had been blown further north than planned, and now the north-westerly winds over this period allowed a more southerly course. Some good sun noon sights with the sextant gave accurate latitudes but getting a good longitude was very difficult, for the navigation tables (despite several plastic bags) were so waterlogged. My hand-held VHF was totally waterlogged, so I could only hope that this southerly course would get the *Kilcullen* back into the shipping lanes, where I might somehow make contact with a passing ship to bring me a fresh food supply and report our position home.

The following day, my worries about food and position seemed to be over, when a small speck appeared on the horizon, and gradually grew bigger and bigger.

'A ship! A ship!' I roared in excitement and started to sing in the early morning sunshine. Visibility was good and the sea was calm so there was little chance of them not seeing the *Kilcullen*. Already I started to taste the fresh fruit, chocolate bars, bread and cheese.

But no; it was not to be. My log entry rather understates the emotional upset I was feeling:

Day 21, 14th August. A container ship *Sharpness* came right on my course. I flared and they still did not see me. Bugger them. This is not fair!

It was early in the morning and visibility was good, with

reasonably calm conditions, so the ship *should* have seen me. I imagine that, miles out in the ocean, nobody was on watch or the watch-keeper was doing other things as the ship steamed along under autopilot. Unfortunately these ultra-modern labour-saving ships are crewed by skeleton staffs, and watch-keeping is not what it used to be. Myself, I would call it downright bad seamanship.

> Day 22, 15th August. Missed another ship this morning. A smoke flare and a parachute flare refused to work. Am running low on flares, with only two left. Have had no luck trying to make contact with the emergency radio either. It's depressing not being seen. I'm worried about Suzanna and friends worrying about me since the *Kilcullen* is overdue. This voyage is daft. There is little point to it save to satisfy my own ends and past failure.

At that stage I was really getting worried about the food supply. While mentally I felt ready to go on for another month if necessary and face likely storms off Ireland and England, without food I would not have the strength to keep going, stay warm and exercise. Unlike the ocean further south, the ocean here was colder and with few fish.

Around about this time I discovered a large can of Andrews Liver Salts in a bag that was outside of my food rationing. Mixed with water, it was a superb refreshing drink like lemonade and I felt fantastic after it. However I simply could not resist the lure of more lemonade and within three hours the entire can of Andrews had disappeared into my stomach. As one can imagine, it totally flushed out my bowels, and my plumbing system was working overtime for the following few days with the runs and subsequent frustration getting through all of those zips in a hurry.

The *Kilcullen*'s fuel supply was all used up save for an emergency supply for a landfall, and the wind had gone very light. It was frustrating not to be making much progress and not being able to stop any ships. I had one smoke flare left and one rocket which simply had to be saved for a life-or-death emergency.

> Day 24, 17th August. The last two days simply did not

exist. Visibility is down to about fifty yards, light wind and no sun. I am just drifting.

During the night of the 16th a ship's engine woke me up. It passed within yards and scared me.

In fact the *Kilcullen* was almost run down; however, as we were such a small, light inflatable I think that the bow wave of a ship would probably have pushed us aside rather than hit us.

My navigation with the plastic sextant was only accurate to about fifty miles and while O.K. for getting direction on the open sea it could be very dangerous for a landfall. By this time I had worked well south and was virtually on a line with the north-west tip of France. So long as it was a landfall, it did not matter where it was, though of course I wanted to make it to Ireland if at all possible.

To come so far and to be lost or wrecked on cliffs or breaking seas off the coast was a real possibility. Indeed few ships come to grief on open sea with plenty of room and it is no accident that most ships go down close to land. With limited manoeuvrability and control, the *Kilcullen* was especially vulnerable.

Shipping was now becoming more frequent and while visibility was poor during the day I would see the lights at night. Several times I saw large trawlers crossing the horizon but I was reluctant to fire my last flares to attract attention, having been disappointed so often. Then one night, clearly on the ocean shelf off Europe, judging by the lines of the trawlers, it seemed that I sailed into the entire Spanish fishing fleet with their bright lights as they fished through the night. Though I wanted to attempt coming alongside one, they were going faster than the *Kilcullen*— even at their slow speeds—and I decided the risk was too great. Not having a good command of their language, I would probably have confused the Spaniards even more.

Day 26, 19th August. I'm tense and hungry but fortunately not cold. I spent a lot of time half sleeping, hallucinating and dreaming. Every so often I wake up as if somebody is calling my name.

I spent a lot of time thinking about the simple things in life we take so much for granted such as a nice cup of tea in fine china, being able to sit in a comfortable armchair and most of all being able to walk down the street and move freely.

Day 27, 20th August. Still have not stopped a ship or trawler, though there are lots of Spaniards about. There are so many of them it's as if they're just sweeping the ocean shelf of fish. Soon there will be none left. Nonetheless I admire the Spanish fishermen—so far from home and living in such primitive conditions.

It blew up last night to near gale force winds and I had to drop all sail. However it eased off this morning and progress is good. I'm impatient.

Not long before noon on August 21st a small coaster appeared on the horizon. It was a difficult decision whether or not to take the risk and fire the last rocket flare to be seen. Fortunately the ship had seen me just as I fired the flare and she altered course. It was an Irish ship, the *Arklow View,* and I roared with joy.

While alone at sea it's one thing talking to yourself and to imaginary people on board with you, but when they start to answer back you have problems. Therefore, as the *Arklow View* grew larger on the horizon, the prospect of human contact after so long was both exciting and terrifying. Undoubtedly the crew were surprised to see me, while I found it a weird experience to talk to real people again. My close, hallucinatory world had been penetrated from the outside.

Arklow View's skipper kindly invited me on board and, much as I would have liked to accept, I'd already learnt that an inflatable comes off very much the worse if it rubs alongside a towering great steel boat, so I kept my distance.

To supplement the rough and ready plot I'd worked out with my last sextant observation, I was very grateful for the position fix I was given by *Arklow View,* which put me equidistant between Milford Haven in Wales and Dunmore East.

Drifting too far south, we had missed our targeted landfall on the west coast of Ireland and sailed right round towards St George's Channel, adding a hundred miles or more to the crossing. Instead of still straining my eyes for sight of land, I might already have been home and dry by now.

With a low-pressure system approaching and the wind forecast to come in from the north-west, *Arklow View*'s skipper suggested that it might be more sensible to head for Wales. However, if at all possible, it was my hope to land in Ireland at Dunmore East, a fishing village on the south-east corner. I did have a small reserve supply of petrol on board, and the brave Suzuki outboard motor was still running: this heartened me in my determination, come hell or high water to make a landfall in Ireland. (Later I was told that if I had landed the *Kilcullen* in England the achievement would have been in the papers much more and would have had much greater recognition in the media. Still, home is home and what you achieve in the long term mattered to me more than quick publicity.)

However, *Arklow View* had reported my position and, in anticipation of a landfall in Wales, the *Daily Express* had flown my wife to Bristol together with our ten-month-old daughter Roisin. I had never said that the *Kilcullen* would land in Wales and it was only some twenty minutes after parting company with the *Arklow View*, having weighed up the risks, that I finally made up my mind in favour of an Irish landfall. Under engine and sail together, I calculated that I had just enough power to take me the fifty miles before the north-westerly gale arrived. This was a risk, but one that I felt was worth taking.

First though, with a fresh supply of food, fruit, biscuits and all sorts of delights, I had a massive feed to the point of making myself sick. My appetite was clearly several times larger than my stomach could cope with after such a long period of rationing. Included in the food supply were boxes of Cornflakes and cartons of long-life milk. On the previous inflatable crossing I had also been given a supply of Cornflakes by a ship; while I was grateful, I could not help thinking that this is a classic example of how life on board a big ship is totally removed from the realities of a tiny craft like mine. With the constant movement it is virtually impossible to hold a plate steady, never mind eating from it without spilling. What one really needs is concentrated nourishment, given the limited space. Though sick in the stomach, frankly I did not care—I could practically smell the land.

As I had no torch working on board, I hastened, before darkness fell, to look up and memorize all the coastal lights—

each could be identified after dark by the number and frequency of flashes. It was once again getting very cold and, seasick as I was, I brought up all my last meal, but at 2026 hrs (GMT) (as my log records) just as darkness approached, I picked up Hook Head, bearing 0020 degrees. Yippee!

'I'll get there by hook or by crook,' exclaimed Oliver Cromwell or so the story goes. He had come to plunder Ireland; all I wanted was to get home. And now Hook Head, Cromwell's dubious inspiration, loomed around the horizon, its lighthouse sending out a powerful flash every three seconds. First established in 1172, Hook Head is said to be one of the oldest working lighthouses in Europe. For me after a month of total isolation on a sixteen-foot inflatable boat, having come through some of the worst North Atlantic storms on record, Hook Head's light was a dream come true.

The reality was painful. My body had degenerated. The salt sores made it virtually impossible to be comfortable and the cold had penetrated to the bone—through several layers of salty damp clothes. It was a case of mind over matter: I didn't mind and nothing mattered more than landing without assistance. To be rescued now would be to fail. It would be a fight to the very end and my determination was cast in concrete.

There was a strong tide flowing. Though the motor was running, there was precious little fuel left and each yard was a struggle, an eternity in itself. Also, the wind was moving around to the north-west with increased strength, and there was no way that the *Kilcullen* could sail into it. The prospect of being blown back out to sea for the next four days, before landing in Wales or England, was too horrible to contemplate. My inner tensions, suppressed through weeks of discomfort, hardship and naked fear, mounted, absurdly combining pain and pure bliss at being so close. Meanwhile, a hundred miles away in Wales, my confused lady wife Suzanna and girlchild Roisin Mairead were expecting me to make a landfall. The *Daily Express* newspaper had planned a champagne reception. I hate the stuff!

I was unsure of the leading navigation lights to the port of Dunmore East, which the *Kilcullen* was making for, but by getting close enough to the loom of the lighthouse it was possible to read the soggy navigation chart. The tide remained foul and twice, on rounding the corner, I nearly came to grief on the rocks. Progress was extremely slow, like the watched kettle that never boils. Then it happened. The quiet and tranquillity, as suddenly everything seemed to stop, was overpowering. The tide was full out, it was four o'clock in the morning and the village of Dunmore slept, oblivious to what was happening in the harbour. I tied up alongside several small boats, hoping that the *Kilcullen* would not be noticed. It was a hard crawl to get up to the quayside. After 28 days in a rubber boat, I had difficulty keeping my balance and could hardly walk; a passer-by might have been excused for considering me a drunkard.

The lone sailor was drunk all right, drunk with joy. Feeling as light as an elephant might in space, he sang and spluttered up the street, parodying Brendan Behan's ballad:

Then the Czar of Russia and the Queen of Prussia
Landed in Dunmore in a big balloon.
They asked the local band to play *The Wearing of the Ocean,*
But the buggers in the bandstand were fast asleep!

This moment had taken eight years to accomplish since I first set out on a calm summer's day from Boston. All I desired in the world now was a pint of Guinness, a telephone call home, a hot bath and crisp dry sheets on a real bed. I was unaware of the amount of interest that the voyage had generated worldwide. I had, after all, left very quietly from Canada. Dunmore is one of the prettiest and most hospitable of ports in all of Ireland. Slowly I staggered up the main street where the Ocean Hotel, run by Brendan Gallagher and his family, is located. There was no reply at the front door. Later I discovered that it was not long since the hotel had gone to bed, following a lively party, and that the Gallaghers' apartment was at the back of the hotel.

In desperation I let myself in and up to the bar for a drink; but it was well secured against lone sailors coming off the Atlantic. In some respects I was worried in case I was committing a crime, but in other ways I simply didn't care as I made my way to the Reception and found a bunch of room keys. I was too exhausted to attempt to work the telephone switch, so I found my way to the bedrooms and on the third attempt found one that was suitable—with a large untenanted double bed made up. This one I settled for and left the other keys back at the Reception with a note to this effect: 'Have been at sea, am a bit wet and cold, have checked myself in—trusting that is O.K.'

I stripped off naked and slipped in between the bed sheets. I've never been to heaven but the sensation is what I've always imagined it to be like. We take the most simple things in life so often for granted and the freedom to stretch out in the bed, having slept in such cramped conditions for so long, was seventh heaven. In a moment I was asleep. It was bliss.

The hotel receptionist was a little late on duty and did not see my note. At daylight my boat had been spotted at the quayside and within minutes it seemed that the entire world's press converged on Dunmore East looking for the lone sailor. The *Kilcullen* was shown on television in the harbour but her skipper could not be found. He was fast asleep.

There were several calls to the hotel who innocently said that I was not there.

On waking I contacted the receptionist and drew attention to my note, oblivious of all the bother going on outside the hotel.

After so many weeks alone I still needed time to readjust even though part of me could not wait to be with Suzanna and Roisin—it never crossed my mind that they could be in Bristol waiting for me to land on that side of the water. But the press was not slow in catching up with me and also I had agreed to talk with the *Daily Express* first about the crossing; they had been good to me and given me some support and I owed them a news story.

The sleep that first night ashore had marked more than just the end of an ocean voyage and the first west-east crossing by inflatable boat. The actual achievement, in many respects, mattered least. It marked my transformation from boyhood to manhood, after a decade of inner conflict. With the burden of failure cast aside on waking, I could make a fresh start, a new beginning with new plans.

I looked over the sparkling silver sea; it looked beautiful and innocent this morning, and I felt a great sense of humility. It is a fool who thinks that he can master the sea.

Appendix I

Kilcullen I and III

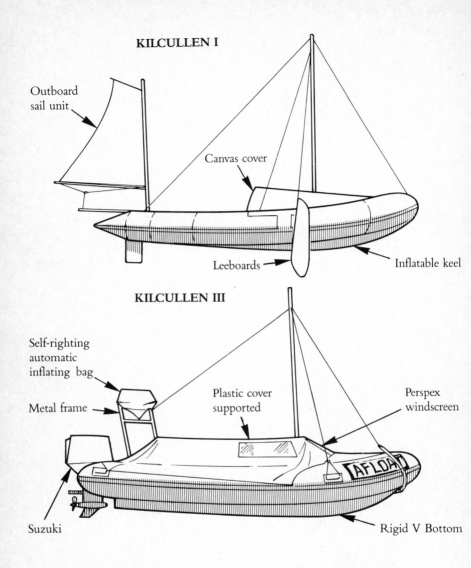

KILCULLEN I

Outboard sail unit

Canvas cover

Leeboards

Inflatable keel

KILCULLEN III

Self-righting automatic inflating bag

Metal frame

Plastic cover supported

Perspex windscreen

Suzuki

AFLOAT

Rigid V Bottom

The self-righting concept with <u>Kilcullen I</u> was to deflate the tubes on one side and to right manually. This was not practicable.

<u>Kilcullen III</u> had an inflatable tube secured to a frame. In an emergency this was inflated by a compressed-air cylinder mounted on the transom, connected to the inflatable tube and engaged by a rip-cord mounted on the transom.

Both dinghies were 16ft (approx.), the principal differences being the self-righting gear and rigid V-shaped hull in <u>Kilcullen III.</u>

APPENDIX I

Kilcullen I and III

Basic equipment carried on *Kilcullen I*

Compass
Camping gas stove
Plastic sextant and tables
Walker Log
Solar still (never used)
Flares and Emergency Position Indicator Beacon
25 gallons petrol
Transistor radio
Spare rudder and leeboards
Torch and batteries
Strobe light
Canned food—varnish-protected for rust
A box full of books—including James Joyce's *Ulysses* and a history of
    Russia.
Survival suit and a bag full of clothes
First Aid kit and survival rations
Repair kit and tool kit

Powered by 6 h.p. outboard motor, outboard sail unit and square sail
    convertible to lateen sail

Basic equipment carried on *Kilcullen III*

Compass
Emergency Seafarer two-way radio
Autohelm by Nautech
Seafarer log
Plastic sextant and tables
Kelvin Hughes satellite navigator
150 gallons of petrol, inflatable tanks
100 Hot Can meals
First Aid kit
Repair kit and tool kit
Flares and emergency rations
Sleeping bag

Survival Suit
Torches and batteries, mast light

Powered by two Suzuki outboard motors, a 55 h.p. and a 9.9 h.p.

The engines proved very reliable while most of the equipment was satisfactory, though during the latter part much was out of commission due to long periods of immersion.

In the fitting out of both dinghies as much simplicity in every way possible was applied. Besides weight and space problems it was also much cheaper!

APPENDIX II

Handling sailing craft up to thirty feet offshore in storm conditions

THE BEST way to handle a small boat in a gale is by staying moored snug in a safe harbour, or by getting to one quick. You can make sure of this by having good navigation information at sea, remaining up to date with weather information, and by watching all the meteorological signs. If you cannot do this there are several excellent books devoted to the subject.

However if you are making a trans-ocean passage or are caught 1,000 miles out into the Atlantic, there is damn all you can do about getting to a safe anchorage or harbour. Also, since most shipwrecks occur close to land, where wave and wind patterns are more unpredictable, very often you have no choice but to head offshore for sea room to ride out the storm.

In the large variety of craft and storms I have been caught out in, the first basic rule I have learned is that there are no rules, just guidelines. With such a variety of sea conditions, craft and crew capacity, there are few cut and dried textbook responses. Rather, you listen to the boat; she will tell you in most cases what to do in addition to using common sense.

In the tragic 1979 Fastnet Race in which fifteen crew members were lost around us, I found myself as a crewman aboard a Ron Holland designed Club Shamrock, *Rapparee.* At 29 feet, she was one of the smallest yachts in the race. While a well rounded team, none of our crew had experience with this *Rapparee,* a modern light-displacement craft, in storm conditions.

At first, with fully reefed sails we tried beating into the rising gale— a method used by larger ocean-racing yachts to drive through gales. The pounding was too great and we could not hold a course into the waves.

Storm jibs are for storms, so up went the storm jib—a tiny sail— with the main dropped and lashed to the deck. We then ran off with the gale. However our speed was so great, introducing the danger of pitchpoling, and the pounding was so severe that the boat said 'Stop!' We felt that if she continued that way she might have broken up.

185

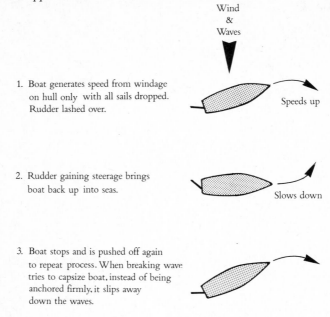

Wind
&
Waves

1. Boat generates speed from windage on hull only with all sails dropped. Rudder lashed over.

Speeds up

2. Rudder gaining steerage brings boat back up into seas.

Slows down

3. Boat stops and is pushed off again to repeat process. When breaking wave tries to capsize boat, instead of being anchored firmly, it slips away down the waves.

Lying a hull

Some other craft our size in that race adopted this tactic, running off before the storm, and came to grief.

We then dropped the storm jib and the boat seemed happiest lying a-hull (see Fig 1), a tactic which I had used with great success on board my 21ft *Kilcullen II* just a month previously through a storm crossing the Bay of Biscay.

At the outset there is an element which seemingly borders on being a coward in adapting this tactic. It is passive, admitting defeat against the storm, securing everything down and going below decks to leave the boat to its own devices. Perhaps; I have no doubt, though, that to survive a storm on the open ocean in a modern light-displacement boat it is the only alternative.

Initially while lying a-hull our skipper wanted to keep a full three-man watch on deck; then a severe knockdown which sent two crew members overboard, only to be saved by their safety harnesses, rapidly changed his mind. The safest place for most on board was below decks lashed into their bunks. One man not in his bunk was hit and hurt by a flying cooker during a severe knockdown.

Quite simply, you must be a coward with the sea. There is no point in being a big hairy-chested man standing up to it. While a crew can hold their own for a period against a storm (perhaps to make a safe harbour), after a period the storm will wear you down and will ultimately win, catching you with your trousers down when you least expect it.

If at all possible you should avoid conflict with the elements, go with them. It is not so much the wind, rather the enormous waves that build up in a storm, that is the enemy. Every so often as weather systems pass, the winds generating the waves will change direction, confusing the seas and occasionally merging waves will grow twice as big as the norm.

On board *Rapparee* in that fatal Fastnet Race we found that the best tactic was to lie a-hull. This is also what I did in several storms on board the 21ft *Kilcullen II.* Sometimes I felt that the smaller boat was even safer! I call it 'the cork principle': go below decks, pop the cork on your Cork Dry Gin, add some tonic, sing a song and the boat will take care of herself, you have done all that you can do. Even in the unlikely event of the boat doing a complete roll, and possibly taking the mast with it, your safest place is secured below.

Most corks have a fat and a thin end. Throw one into some waves and watch it bob up and down slipping away from the waves. Instead of fighting the wind and waves you simply bounce up and down to slip away from them. In an older heavy long-keeled yacht this rule does not necessarily apply. She will be more firmly anchored to the waves and you are likely to suffer more damage. Though I have little direct experience with craft such as this, the most sensible option is, it seems, to run off before the seas.

On board my two inflatables crossing the Atlantic—that is *Kilcullen I* (the flat bottomed Zodiac) and *Kilcullen III,* also 16 feet long with a rigid V bottom—in severe storms I adopted the same tactic, while taking on water ballast in the severest conditions. This way capsize was avoided.

The reason for my capsize in *Kilcullen I* was because, in an easterly storm blowing me away from the west coast of Ireland, the *Kilcullen* was lying bow into the wind and waves and held by sea-anchors, but the lines holding the sea-anchors snapped.

Kilcullen III's capsize came for different reasons. While still alert and in control during the early part of the storm, I was running off before it, making progress in the desired direction, negotiating each wave as it came. As the storm persisted and the waves grew I became more tired and misjudged a wave while going into the lying a-hull survival mode. My mistake was in not making this move earlier. Fortunately, unlike in the first *Kilcullen,* I was more prepared for that capsize.

Getting back to general theory on surviving a storm, there are many wrong and outdated views expressed regarding the best ways to survive. With some notable exceptions, many still refer to the old out-of-date classic textbooks. Also what applies to larger and older craft does not necessarily apply to smaller craft.

Essentially there are five ways often discussed to survive a storm. I now list them in order of importance and effectiveness based on my views and direct experience. In all situations it is assumed that at this stage you have dropped all sail and have everything lashed securely.

1) Lying a-hull—the cork principle

Most recommended and discussed above. Lash the helm over, and stay secured below. In a severe storm with confused and big seas you run a greater risk of being capsized and there may be more discomfort than running off before it, but this is infinitely better than going head over heels.

2) Running off downwind

This is O.K. if you are in full control with a reliable crew and can remain alert to negotiate each wave or if the storm is not too severe.

3) Trailing warps

A tactic sometimes advocated, running off before a storm downwind, the idea being to slow your craft down. This is O.K. to a point; however in severe waves you are holding the boat against the storm and, at some stage, an enormous wave will lift everything up in a heap, creating an enormous jerk and another heave leading to a possible pitchpole and great damage from the sea.

4) Sea-anchors

Not recommended. The same applies as with trailing warps.

5) Spreading oil on the water

A joke. Useful only if you have an oil tanker on standby or perhaps if you wish to calm the sea temporarily if you have to recover a man overboard.

Above all else, use common sense and stay secured to your boat; you have a much greater chance of making it through this way than in a liferaft. Listen to your boat, she will tell you how to behave.

In the storm that brought the end of *Kilcullen II,* due to a totally different set of circumstances, we owed our survival to staying with the boat right to the very last moment while the liferaft was torn to pieces on the jagged rocks.

APPENDIX III

Inflatable liferafts and survival

THERE is an illustration depicting Assur-Nasir-Pal and his army crossing a river using inflated devices, circa B.C. 880 (Nimrud Gallery, British Museum). The like is still done today by the Tibetans and Chinese on the Huang Ho river, 28 centuries later. However it was only during the Second World War and the early 1950s with the development of modern materials that inflatable liferafts have come into their own. For this reason, as a relatively new development, we still have a great deal to learn. Modern satellite emergency communications facilities are all very well but the oceans remain an enormous anonymous chunk covering two thirds of this world of ours.

The traditional school of thought with liferaft design is that they are passive in concept. That is, when your ship goes down, you stay in the one area awaiting rescue. In certain circumstances that is all very well for larger craft. I believe in the active concept: you aim to be self-sufficient and make your own way to safety or rescue.

The problem is that most small-craft liferaft design comes from bigger ocean vessels who follow defined ocean routes. (Unless you apply their rules, for example, you may not get insurance.) This is very often not the case with small pleasure craft increasingly crossing oceans and sailing to more remote places. Hence the concept of the sailing liferaft. Then you have the choice either to stay close to the scene of the disaster if you think the chance of rescue is greater, or alternatively to head for the safety of land or to where there is more shipping traffic, if far out into the ocean.

Curiously, for self-rescue, at this time of writing, there are few suitable craft that are tailor-made for yachtsmen. Experience has shown that models developed for small-boat sailors very often fall short in expectations, equipment and design.

In survival terms we only hear of those who made it after getting into difficulties; invariably it is those who have done something to sail themselves to safety or rescue. A classic story is one which occurred on 15 June 1972 to the Robinson family. Their yacht was suddenly sunk by a killer whale; there were six on board. At first they went for their inflatable liferaft which, like most compact light rafts on modern yachts, was a flimsy affair. Fortunately it inflated, but after seventeen days it had to be abandoned because of air leaks. What saved the Robinsons

189

was an additional 9ft GRP dinghy equipped with an inflatable collar. In all, 37 days after being shipwrecked, the exhausted Robinsons were picked up having voyaged 750 miles towards a landfall.

In another example, during their epic survival of 117 days, Maurice and Maralyn Bailey had an Avon liferaft with a small Avon inflatable dinghy. Happily both craft survived, but their dinghy was in far better shape than their liferaft.

As far back as 1952, Dr Alain Bombard's exploits crossing the Atlantic on the warmer southerly east–west route, and my own exploits going the other way, show that properly equipped inflatables can be used as survival craft.

Another survival example of self-rescue is that of American Steve Callahan—a participant in the same race I completed, the Mini-Transat single-handed Atlantic event. Steve lost his boat some time out of the Canaries en route to the West Indies. Alone in his raft, there was zero chance of beating back into the prevailing trade winds. Instead he drifted and, at times, pulled up the anchor pockets of his conventional liferaft in an attempt to sail to rescue.

Steve's survival story, told in his book *Adrift,* is remarkable. On the subject of sailing liferafts, he said that had he been able to beam reach to the Cape-Verde Islands with a proper sailing rig he could have shortened his ordeal and voyage to safety from 1,800 miles to 450 miles.

'Had I been able to travel at an average speed of 3 knots, even if only downwind to the West Indies, my survival voyage would have lasted only 25 days rather than 76. Had I been able both to reach and to maintain a speed of three knots, my voyage would have lasted a mere six and a quarter days,' Steve added.

The ideal solution in my view is a general-purpose robust inflatable dinghy. Inherent in its design should be an ability to ride out storms and a capability to provide the means of sailing towards the best chance of rescue when conditions allow. For the small-boat sailor, this sort of tough tender on which you could fit a CO_2 cylinder for emergency inflation during offshore passages—with your own hand-made survival kit—would seem a cost-efficient answer to survival.

The alternative is an expensive wasted, flimsy, lightweight and compact raft in a sealed box or bag which you are not even sure will work when needed. To check it out at all is an expensive exercise running into hundreds of pounds; even the survival pack may not suit the area you wish to sail. Likewise very often the temptation is to skip the liferaft servicing for a year or so, thinking sure, it will never happen to me... Another consideration, of course, is that if cruising remote parts of the world, it simply may not be possible to get service.

While the purpose of this appendix is not as a definitive survival guide, rather some practical tips from my experiences, let us now assume that everything has gone wrong. Inherent here is the principle that your boat is the best liferaft you could ever have. If you don't accept this, read the 1979 Fastnet Race report. Nobody who managed to stay with their boat perished—even if the craft was dismasted, waterlogged and reduced to a hulk. By contrast, several who took to their liferafts, which subsequently broke up, were lost.

By this stage you will either have drowned, died from exposure, or made it to your liferaft, one which preferably can sail. It goes without saying that your rescue craft and all safety equipment must be located at an easily accessible location during offshore passages. It is too lazy a mode to adopt the attitude: sure, it could never happen to me.

Of all the survival situations I have been in—and had the misfortune to get myself into—there is one clear-cut common denominator: Never give up. This applies to all who come through difficult situations. In our daily lives we very often give up, sometimes simply because we do not want something badly enough. The ultimate animal instinct we have for survival is all-powerful and ruthless.

Going with this is having the confidence to know that you, and all with you, can survive. People have asked me several times, did I ever think there was a time that I would not make it. Quite simply no, while this may have indeed been the situation, to admit it at the time would have been a self-fulfilling prophecy. Alone it is more difficult but the same applies if you are with a group. Somebody has to lead and make it clear that the team can make it.

During the survival tests by the U.S. Navy one subject, unbriefed on what to expect and do in water at forty degrees F., was crying in genuine agony after three and a half minutes and had to be hauled out; whereas a second subject, already briefed, endured the same temperature for forty minutes, swimming gently until almost unconscious. The clear conclusion here is that attitude and indoctrination in these matters is important. The old well worn phrase, stating that where there is a will there is a way, holds good.

On a practical side, now that attitude is sorted out and one assumes a reasonable level of common sense, and you find yourself alone or with a crew in a liferaft, let us assume that, depending on your liferaft, as discussed above, you have decided to adopt active or passive survival tactics.

Regardless, the first major obstacle is likely to be seasickness. In my case I had been at sea in a tiny craft for 46 days and yet, on climbing into the raft, I became very sick. This drains energy and, as in other circumstances where one becomes seasick, take extreme care not to do anything irrational. Stay huddled up, force yourself to move with greater caution and conserve energy.

While in warmer waters sun stroke and exposure to the sun is a danger, then the cold at night time when everything adjusts to water temperature is a great danger, and becomes more acute the further north one moves in the northern hemisphere or the reverse down south.

While loaded down by several layers of clothing, wet to the skin, my greatest friend and life-saving device has been isometric exercises. That is, the systematic tensioning of muscles in your body; you can actually exercise without moving. In my own case I would have further aggravated salt sores and soft skin blisters by movement for exercise. However by isometric exercises, tensioning a limb at a time, or sometimes my whole body, I could warm up and concentrate the mind. Indeed, through the long hours of darkness, merged with day, I would concentrate on isometrics, warm up, become tired and drop off to sleep to awake about half an hour later cold and miserable to repeat the exercise. Of course my one big worry in the cold was that I would not wake up out of it and continue on in a trance beyond a point of no return. It took sheer willpower and determination to keep mind and body pulling together.